HOW CAN YOU BE SURE?

*Charles Stanley and John Wesley
Debate Salvation and Security*

by
MARK BIRD, D.MIN.

SCHMUL PUBLISHING CO.

SCHMUL'S WESLEYAN BOOK CLUB   SALEM, OHIO

All scripture quotations unless otherwise indicated are taken from the King James Version. Permission to quote from the following copyrighted versions of the Bible is acknowledged with appreciation:

The *New American Standard Bible* (NAS), © the Lockman Foundation, 1960, 1962, 1968, 1971, 1972, 1973, 1975.

The *New King James Version* (NKJ), copyright © 1979, 1980, 1982 by Thomas Nelson, Inc.

Published by Schmul Publishing Co.
PO Box 716
Salem, Ohio USA

Printed in the United States of America

ISBN 0-88019-483-9

Contents

Acknowledgements

I want to thank all of those who have contributed to this book by reading the manuscript and giving me suggestions that I have incorporated into the book. I thank my wife, Kristin; my seminary professors Dr. Gareth Cockerill and Dr. Steve Flick; my colleagues Dr. Steve Gibson and Dr. Philip Brown; my mentors Rev. Larry Grile and Dr. Mike Williams; my students from Systematic Theology class, particularly Ty Brewer, Mark Mander, Jonathon Phillips, Joey Ratcliff, and Paul Wolfe; and my "Calminian" friend Dr. Dan Harting, who disagrees with much of Stanley's theology. *I* take responsibility for any of the book's flaws.

HOW CAN YOU BE SURE?
Charles Stanley and John Wesley
Debate Salvation and Security

FOREWORD

In this book, Dr. Mark Bird provides all thoughtful students of the Christian faith an astute study in comparative theology—especially in the area of soteriology. The comparison is between Charles Stanley, a popular and very influential contemporary radio and television preacher, and John Wesley, who, for the holiness churches, still provides the benchmark standard.

Generally the belief in unconditional eternal security is traced to the foundational doctrines provided by hyper-Calvinism, primarily predestination and limited atonement. Bird rather traces Stanley's vehement position to his peculiar understandings of grace, the atonement, God's omnipotence and sovereignty, and especially on God's unconditional love.

Stanley was originally an Arminian and adopted belief in eternal security while a seminarian. Clearly he did not shed as much of his Arminianism as he thought, for in his system he says little about predestination and vigorously claims to believe in a universal atonement.

Considering the fact that along with unlimited racial availability, he sees the atonement as objective, in the sense that all sins, past, present and future are covered, *penally*, it is difficult to see how he can escape the implication of universalism.

As one follows Dr. Bird's clear and competent exposition of Stanley's defense of Eternal Security, one gradually comes to see that Stanley's thinking is beset by two fundamental errors. First is his unbiblical and illogical stress on unconditional love. This seems to be the kingpin of his thought. The amazing illogic is his acceptance of John 3:16 with its condition, "that whoever believes in him" (NIV). Here is love for the world with a condition built into the very heart of it. If God so loved the whole world that He gave His Son to save it, then one would think that He would save it, well, *unconditionally*. From a Wesleyan standpoint, to add "faithful obedience" and "perseverance" to the mix no more compromises God's love than does the "believing."

The other fatal error is in supposing that a penal atonement must be absolute: it cannot be provisional without ceasing to be penal. But as Bird makes clear, John Wesley refused to allow himself to be impaled on the horns of this dilemma.

The sum of the matter is that while Charles Stanley would eschew antinomianism in theory, he opens the door wide to its rankest practice.

One comes away from this erudite work with the comforting conviction that John Wesley, after all, is the safest teacher—more biblical, more logical, and far more consistent with the great historical tenets of the Christian faith.

—RICHARD S. TAYLOR, TH.D.
Covina, California

INTRODUCTION

W hen I was younger, I had one wish, like Solomon had. I wished that I knew I was saved," said a Seventh Day Adventist boy I talked to recently. Like this boy, who is still confused about the issue, many other people long for an assurance of salvation. Security is a universal emotional need.

Both of the men whose names grace the cover of this book, Charles Stanley and John Wesley, longed for and experienced an assurance of personal salvation. Wesley learned that it was the great privilege of every believer to know that he is *now* saved. He taught that a Christian could know this by believing God's Word and experiencing the witness of the Spirit (with confirmation through the fruit of the Spirit). On the other hand, Charles Stanley bases his assurance primarily on the doctrine of unconditional eternal security. He teaches that one can know that he is eternally secure in Christ, regardless of any future choices he might make.

Who is right? If I can know I am saved, does that mean I can know I could never be lost? Or does it mean that I can have a

Charles Stanley:	**John Wesley:**
"I know from experience that until you settle once and for all the question of whether or not you are eternally secure... joy will elude you."	"About a quarter before nine...I felt my heart strangely warmed. I felt I did trust in Christ, Christ alone for salvation; and an assurance was given me that He had taken away my sins."

present assurance of salvation and a confidence that Jesus will keep me as long as I "keep myself in the love of God?" We could hardly overestimate the importance of this question. Most well-known radio preachers teach unconditional eternal security. Most popular books on theology teach unconditional eternal security. But most classical theologians and many modern theologians would call this doctrine into question.

In this book, Charles Stanley, a popular and influential pastor/teacher, and John Wesley, a classical theologian and revivalist, will "debate" foundational doctrines relating to this issue. We will not deal with this subject by simply looking at proof texts on either side of the debate. Those who believe in unconditional eternal security say that their belief is not simply derived from a few proof texts, but is based on several key doctrines. They say that a proper understanding of the nature of faith, works, repentance, grace, salvation, sanctification, the atonement, etc. result in a belief that once one is saved, he can never be lost. In this book, we will see how Charles Stanley and John Wesley treat these doctrines. With the help of these men, we will examine these foundational doctrines to see if they indeed should lead one to conclude that eternal security is unconditional and that our personal assurance of salvation should be based on that belief.

Why has Stanley been chosen to represent the "unconditional eternal security" position? Though he doesn't represent all Calvinists, Neo-Calvinists, or "Calminians," he is a popular, influential pastor who represents a large segment of the evangelical world. He is a well-respected leader[1] seeking to help people grow in grace according to biblically-based principles. Stanley pastors a large Southern Baptist church in Atlanta, Georgia (14,000 members at its peak) and has much influence through his effective In Touch Ministries (speaking on both radio and television) and his many books. One of those books is *Eternal Security, Can You Be Sure?* It is this popular book that we will primarily use to analyze Stanley's theology. In *Eternal Security* Stanley does a Herculean job attempting to demonstrate the necessary connection between unconditional eternal security and the doctrines he feels support it.[2] But the question is: Does a proper understanding of those doctrines really support unconditional eternal security, or have those doctrines been tailored to make them more consistent with unconditional eternal security?

John Wesley, the other "debater," represents a historic Christianity that rejected both Hypercalvinism and Roman Catholicism, two forms of Christianity quite different from the Christianity of the first four centuries. John Wesley, a *via media* Anglican and founder of the Methodist movement, had more knowledge of and reverence for the consensual thought of the church fathers than most in his or our generation. He had a genius for reconciling seemingly conflicting doctrines and bringing balance to evangelical Christianity. Wesley found himself between what he thought were the extremes of antinomianism (which he thought Calvinism mothered) and pharisaism (found in much of the Roman Catholic Church, and even in the Church of England, mediated by Pelagian Arminianism). Though attacked on either side by the antinomians and by the legalists, Wesley was used by God to lead one of the greatest evangelical revivals of all time. One of his primary contributions to the Christian world was his emphasis of the doctrine of assurance. Wesley said that the doctrine of the witness of the Spirit (giving assurance of salvation) was "one grand part" of the testimony which God had given the Methodists to bear to all mankind.

> Every important doctrine has eternal consequences.

This book deals with basic Christian doctrines with potential practical implications. Every important doctrine works itself out in real life and even has eternal consequences. For example, certain doctrines lead to antinomianism. If antinomianism ultimately proves to be a false theology, many will suffer forever as a result of believing those erroneous doctrines. Some doctrines lead to works-righteousness. If works-righteousness ultimately proves to be a false theology, many will suffer forever as a result of believing those erroneous doctrines. Likewise, the doctrine of assurance and its underlying doctrines have eternal consequences.

Admittedly, this book is written by a Wesleyan Arminian. Much evaluation will be a critique of Stanley's theology. However, I believe I have been faithful to the writings of both Stanley and Wesley and fair in my analysis.

Enjoy the debate!

Endnotes

1. When Protestants were asked in a study to name the three most important leaders in the country, seventy-two percent of respondents included Billy Graham, thirteen percent included James Dobson, eight percent included their own pastors, Charles Swindoll and Charles Colson were each named by seven percent, Charles Stanley and Pope John Paul II were each named by six percent, and Mother Teresa and Pat Robertson were each named by four percent. "World News," *Moody*, March/April, 1996, p. 40.

2. Stanley, once an Arminian, converted to Neo-Calvinistic dispensational theology while at Southwestern Theological Seminary. Charles Stanley, *Eternal Security, Can You Be Sure?* (Nashville: Thomas Nelson, 1990), pp. 2-3.

1: SIN

CAN SIN SEPARATE THE UNFAITHFUL FROM GOD?

One's understanding of sin has a tremendous effect on one's understanding of salvation. This chapter shows how Stanley's and Wesley's views of sin help determine their view of the believer's security. We will present Stanley's view, then Wesley's, and then compare the two. Though we will note several similarities between Stanley and Wesley, it would be hard to overstate the difference between Wesley and Stanley regarding the effects of sin in a believer's life.

Stanley on Sin

Stanley believes that Adam was responsible for sin entering into the human race. When Adam fell by disobeying God, sin and its consequences passed to all men. *Every* man, woman, and child since Adam was born in sin.[1] The condition of man today is that he is a child of wrath as a result of Adam's sin. He is the enemy of God. He is ungodly and a sinner.[2]

Stanley believes that one is a sinner in two ways—by his nature and by his actions. Though sin is exhibited by one's actions, man's

---

Stanley:	Wesley:
If one trusts in Christ, sin will never again separate him from God.	Sin destroys faith, and faith is necessary for salvation.

---

basic problem is his nature. Sin has contaminated man's nature. As a result of the fall of Adam, man is born with an inclination toward evil, a bias away from good. Stanley says, "If you don't believe me, ask any preschool worker or kindergarten teacher. Children never need a lesson in being bad. It comes naturally."[3] Each child eventually demonstrates his evil inclination, which is described by Stanley as a defiant self-centeredness willing to challenge any and all authority.[4] Sin is rebellion.[5]

Because the evil nature leads a person to commit acts of disobedience, he experiences not only *sin* but *sins* as well. The *sin* a person experiences is that inclination toward evil that results from his relation with Adam. The *sins* one experiences result from his personal disobedience.[6]

The combination of one's inherent sinfulness and one's sins puts him under condemnation from God. One is guilty (under condemnation) for both the sin inherited from Adam and the sins of his actions.[7] This condemnation results in separation from God. Man is

> **Stanley:**
> One is guilty for both the sin inherited from Adam and personal sins.

separated from God now and potentially for eternity because of his sin. One must remember that when the Bible says that the wages of sin is death, it is not referring to annihilation, but separation from God. If one dies physically while still separated from God spiritually, he will exist eternally apart from God.[8]

The reason sin separates man from God is that God is holy and those who have fellowship with Him must be holy as well. They must be guiltless, guilty of no sin whatsoever. God's nature demands this.[9] God's nature also demands that sin be penalized by death. The only hope for mankind then was that God placed the sin of man on His Son, who died for that sin, paying its penalty.[10]

Jesus' dying on the cross didn't automatically cure the sin problem, however. He did pay the debt for the sin of man, but in order for a person to be reconciled to God, that person must meet the one requirement for salvation—believe on the One who had died in his place. Even though Christ died for everyone, one will go to hell if he doesn't take advantage of the provision of the cross. In other words, if one refuses to believe in Christ, he will forever be separated from God because of his sin.[11]

But Stanley must not be misunderstood here. Since Christ has already paid the penalty for sin and since He only requires belief in Christ to be saved, then it takes more than sinning to keep one out of heaven:

> We must understand exactly what sends a person to hell. As we have seen, sin alone is not enough. Heaven will be full of people who committed all kinds of sin. It takes more than simply sinning to get to hell.
>
> It is not lying, cheating, stealing, raping, murdering, or being unfaithful that sends people to hell. It is rejecting Christ, refusing to put their trust in Him for the forgiveness of sin.[12]

Stanley is saying that the only sin that will send anyone to hell is the sin of not believing on Christ—the sin of unbelief. Sin against God (other than not accepting His Son) will not keep one out of heaven, since Christ paid for everyone's sins on the cross. Stanley goes on to make his point clear: If one has accepted Christ, he will go to heaven regardless of the number or severity of the sins he commits, even if he never repents of them.[13]

Thus the consequence of sin is spiritual death, but only if one refuses to exercise a single act of faith in Christ. One need not *continue* to believe in Christ to escape spiritual death.[14] If one does trust in Christ, sin, no matter how severe, will never again separate him from God. Sin might destroy fellowship with God, but never the relationship. Sin may forfeit one's reward in Heaven but never Heaven itself. Though it is possible for Christians to sin (and they often will) it is not possible for Christians to lose their salvation by sinning.[15]

> **Stanley:**
> The only sin that will send anyone to hell is the sin of unbelief.

Wesley on Sin

Wesley believed that all men are born in sin as a result of Adam's disobedience in the Garden. Though both Adam and Eve sinned, Adam is responsible for sin entering into the world since he is the representative of mankind. All mankind are affected by Adam to the extent that by his fall, they all have fallen into sorrow, pain, and death, both spiritual and physical.[16]

Man was created originally in the image of God—in the natural, political, and moral image of God. The natural image was a picture of God's own immortality. Man was made a spiritual being, given understanding, free will, and various affections. The political image was man's right to have dominion over the earth. The moral image means that, like God, man was full of love, justice, mercy, and truth. And as God is holy and pure, so was man. But when man fell, he lost the moral image of God, and lost partially the natural image of God.[17]

As the consequence of the fall, all men are by nature dead in trespasses and sins, without hope, without God in the world, and therefore children of wrath. They are apart from the life and the image of God. In man's natural state, he has no love for God and no fear of God. All men naturally are idolaters; if they don't worship nature or man-made idols, they worship themselves. All men naturally love their own will—they are self-willed.

They also love the world. They seek the lust of the eye, the lust of the flesh, and the pride of life (I John 2:15-16). Men are conceived in sin and "shapen in wickedness." The carnal mind in every man so infects the whole soul that there dwells in him, in his natural state, no good thing, but every imagination of the thoughts of his heart is only evil continually (Gen. 6:5). Man is naturally inwardly depraved. Wesley believed that this doctrine of original sin or inherited depravity is the fundamental point which distinguishes heathenism from Christianity. Anyone who denies this fact of the inward total depravity of man is still a heathen.[18]

Wesley taught that, naturally, man is so depraved inwardly that his will is free only to do evil. The only reason that anyone is able to choose Christ or perform any "duty" is that "every man has a measure of free will restored to him by grace."[19]

Wesley distinguished between this inward depravity and acts of sin. When someone is saved, he is forgiven of past acts of sin, but inward depravity still remains until one is entirely sanctified.[20]

Wesley also made a distinction between acts of sins. He divided acts of sin into categories of sins "properly so-called"— which are willful transgressions against known laws of God, acts of rebellion—and sins "improperly so-called," which are involuntary transgressions of a law of God, known or unknown.[21] Wesley called some sins "improperly so-called" because he believed that the usual way the Bible and Christians use the word "sin" is as a willful transgression (when it refers to an act), although "sin" can be used to designate any transgression against a law of God, whether willful or not.

Wesley divided acts of sin in two other ways: sins of omission vs. sins of commission (or negative sins vs. positive sins) and inward sins vs. outward sins.[22] Sins of omission usually precede sins of commission and inward sins usually precede outward sins.

Sin is what brings condemnation to the soul, and thus separation from God. Man is separated from God by sin since God is holy and cannot tolerate sin. The only way man could be reconciled to God is through the atonement made by Christ on the cross.

Man is guilty of all willful sins that he has committed as a result of yielding to the inherited inclination to sin. (Because of grace, individuals are not counted as guilty for inherited depravity.[23]) The guilt from willful sin brings separation from God. One must be born again to be freed of this guilt and be reconciled to God. Once one is born again by faith in Christ, he must continue to trust in Christ in order to continue to be free of guilt. Since willful sin destroys faith, one must be careful not to disobey God.[24] Willful sin will bring condemnation to a soul after one is saved just as it brought condemnation before salvation (Hebrews 10:26-27). Grace and willful sin are not compatible, though one does have an Advocate if he does sin (I John 2:1). It is possible for one to forfeit his salvation through willful sin—rebellion against God.

> **Wesley:**
> Grace and sin are not compatible.

One of the ways that Wesley perceived "backsliding" to take place may be outlined as follows:

1. A Christian is tempted.
2. The Spirit warns him.
3. The man gives in a little.
4. The Spirit is grieved, and faith is weakened.

5. The Spirit reproves the person.

6. The man turns away from the voice of God.

7. Evil desire begins and spreads in the person's soul until faith and love vanish away.

8. He is now capable of committing outward sin.[25]

Wesley believed that a person would usually destroy his faith with *inward* sin before he would commit an *outward* sin.[26]

Evaluation

Please see comparison chart, page 20, to better understand the following evaluation.

Charles Stanley and John Wesley both have a traditional understanding of inherited depravity. They also both believe that the only solution to the sin problem (depravity and acts of sin) is Jesus Christ. Beyond that, however, there is a lot of discrepancy between our two debaters, as you can see from the chart. Wesley has the more coherent understanding of the nature of sin, while Stanley has a few logical inconsistencies to deal with.

Stanley insists that sin cannot separate someone from God once he becomes a Christian. Only unbelief (never accepting Christ) can keep one from heaven. Jesus paid for all sin; therefore no sin except unbelief can keep anyone separated from God. But if failing to believe in Christ is the only sin that could keep us separated from God, what about babies who die, never having had a chance to believe? If we say that babies are provisionally saved prior to the age of accountability, then it is their first act of willful sin that revokes their provisional salvation and separates them from God. If willful sin is what brings someone under condemnation, how can we then say that unbelief is the only thing that could send a person to hell?

Stanley's view becomes even more problematic when unbelief is rightfully considered a sin. If all sin, including unbelief, is paid for in the sense that Stanley says sin is paid for, then why isn't everyone saved? Since Stanley does not believe in a limited atonement, he has a real theological dilemma here.

Even if it could be argued that unbelief is the only sin that keeps one from heaven, then why does Stanley deny that unbelief condemns

Sin	Stanley	Wesley
On Depravity	Adam was responsible for sin entering the human race. All persons are born with inherited depravity and thus are all children of wrath. This depravity or inclination to evil is a defiant self-centeredness.	*Same as Stanley*
On Sin and Prevenient Grace	Stanley doesn't mention prevenient grace, or common grace, the term used by Calvinists to refer to the grace God gives even to sinners to keep them from sinning as much as they would otherwise.	Because of the depth of inherited depravity, no one can do any good except through prevenient grace—a divine enabling.
On Guilt	All persons are not only guilty for the sins they commit but also for inherited depravity.	All persons are guilty only for the sins they commit.
On the Only Solution to Sin	Sin brings condemnation and thus separation from God and ultimately eternal death unless the blood of Christ intervenes. The only hope the human race has is through the atoning death of Christ. The reason we need Christ is that the nature of God demands that those He allows into heaven be holy. We can only be made holy through Christ.	*Same as Stanley*
On What Will Keep People Out of Heaven	Since the atonement cancels past, present and future sins, it takes more than sinning to miss heaven; what it takes to miss heaven is to fail to believe in Christ.	Because the atonement has not canceled out all sin automatically, willful sin is still what will keep unrepentant souls out of heaven.
On the Distinction Between Kinds of Sin	There is a difference between sin as depravity and sin as acts.	There is a distinction between depravity and sinful acts, and a distinction between "sins properly so-called," and "sins improperly so-called." We are culpable only for "sins properly so-called," or willful sins.
On Sin's Effect After Salvation	Personal willful sin cannot separate one from God after salvation though it did before salvation.	Personal willful sin can separate one from God even after salvation by destroying faith.

those who fall back into unbelief after they are saved?[27] Hebrews 3:12-14 warns, "Beware, brethren, lest there be in any of you an evil heart of unbelief in departing from the living God; but exhort one another daily, while it is called "Today," lest any of you be hardened through the deceitfulness of sin. For we have become partakers of Christ if we hold the beginning of our confidence steadfast to the end" (NKJ). This passage teaches that we can depart from God in unbelief, having been hardened by the deceitfulness of sin. Only those who keep their faith to the end will enter heaven.

As we have begun to see, Stanley's view of sin is based on his view of the atonement. In chapter three this will become more obvious. In the meantime, we can see that Stanley's view of sin opens wide the door to lawlessness.

John Wesley is helpful on this subject for making important distinctions between kinds of sin. It is personal willful sin that condemns us, not inherited depravity or sins of ignorance (which Wesley termed "sins improperly-so-called"). Wesley is also helpful in pointing out that willful sin destroys the faith that is necessary for continued salvation. He made it clear that willful sin after salvation is still deadly — it still can damn the unfaithful. Unlike Stanley's view, Wesley's view of the atonement does not weaken the effect of willful sin in the believer's life.

Though Wesley's teaching on "backsliding" may not exactly fit the experience of many Christians who have fallen, his position is much stronger than Stanley's. Stanley's position can have very negative practical implications. If one believes that there are no choices he might make that could keep him from heaven, he might begin to carelessly disregard the laws of God.

Endnotes:

1. Charles Stanley, *Eternal Security, Can You Be Sure?* (Nashville: Thomas Nelson, 1990), p. 27.

2. Tape 1, in a tape series called *Eternal Security, Can You Be Sure?* By Charles Stanley, copyright 1990 by In Touch Ministries. The message on tape one is entitled: "Where it All Begins." The tape series will be referred to in the rest of this book in the following format: Tape #, Message, *Eternal Security.*

3. *Eternal Security,* p. 27.

4. Ibid., p. 27.

5. Tape 1, "Where it All Begins," *Eternal Security.*

6. *Eternal Security*, p. 27.

7. Ibid.

8. Ibid., p. 29.

9. Ibid.

10. See chapter three for a discussion of the atonement.

11. Ibid., p. 67.

12. Ibid., p. 70.

13. Ibid., p. 71. This is true in Stanley's theology because for him the only thing necessary to meet the sole condition of faith is a single act of faith (in a moment of time). Faith does not need to be maintained. See chapter four.

14. Ibid., p. 80.

15. Ibid., pp. 70, 71.

16. Thomas Jackson, ed., *The Works of the Rev. John Wesley, A.M.*; with the Last Corrections of the Author. 3rd ed., 14 vol., (London: Wesleyan-Methodist Book Room, 1829-31) "The Doctrine of Original Sin," 9:332.

17. Wesley seemed to believe that the moral image could be completely restored in this life. He said, "By nature ye are wholly corrupted: by grace ye shall be wholly renewed. In Adam ye all died; in the second Adam, in Christ, ye all are made alive... Go on from faith to faith until your whole sickness be healed, and all that mind be in you, which was also in Christ Jesus!" *Works*: "Original Sin," 6:65.

18. "Is man by nature filled with all manner of evil? Is he void of all good? Is he wholly fallen? ... Allow this, and you are so far a Christian. Deny it, and you are but an Heathen still." *Works:* "Original Sin," 6:63.

19. *Works*: "Some Remarks on Mr. Hill's Review..." 10:392.

20. *Works*: "On Working Out Our Own Salvation," 6:509.

21. John Wesley, *A Plain Account of Christian Perfection.* (Kansas City: Beacon Hill, 1966), p.54. In the sermon "The Great Privilege of Those That Are Born Again," Wesley defined sin as it is used in I John 5: "By sin, I here understand outward sin, according to the plain, common acceptation of the word; an actual, voluntary transgression of the law; of the revealed, written law of God; of any commandment of God, acknowledged to be such at the time that it is transgressed." *Works*: 5:227.

22. *Works*: "The Great Privilege of Those That Are Born of God," 5:230-2.

23. G. Osborne, collector, *The Poetical Works of John and Charles Wesley, 13 vols.* (London: Wesleyan-Methodist Conference Office, 1868-72), "Free Grace," 3:93.

24. *Works*: "The Great Privilege of Those That Are Born of God," 5:231-232.

25. Ibid., 5:231.

26. Ibid., 5:232.

27. *Eternal Security*, p. 80.

2: GRACE AND THE NATURE OF GOD

How Do the Attributes of God Affect His Offer of Grace?

Does God's love mean that He offers His grace unconditionally? Can God's holiness allow one to sin and still be a Christian? Can God be sovereign if man can forfeit the salvation that God intended he should have? These and other important questions that concern the relationship between the nature of God and the offer of grace will be the focus of this chapter. One might be amazed to find that Stanley and Wesley, though both evangelicals, are widely separated in their concept of the nature of God as it relates to the offer of grace.

Stanley's View of Grace and the Nature of God

God's Love

Stanley believes that God offers unconditional love to all who will accept it by faith. A person's expression of faith places him in an unconditional relationship with the Heavenly Father.[1] God's love for His children is unconditional—there are absolutely no conditions at-

---

Charles Stanley:
"If abandoning the faith or falling into sin short-circuits salvation, I have the ability to demonstrate unconditional love to a greater extent than God."

John Wesley:
"The God of love is willing to save all the souls that He has made. He leaves it up to them."

---

tached to the love of God for His children. This means that once a person becomes a Christian, he can do nothing that would separate himself from the salvation he has already received, even if he abandons his faith in Christ.[2] God's unconditional love will keep his salvation intact. If there were something that one had to do to remain a Christian or if there were something one could do to lose his salvation, that would mean that God's love is not unconditional.[3]

If one could forfeit his salvation, humans would have the capacity to love unconditionally better than God:

> If abandoning the faith or falling into sin short-circuits salvation, I have the ability to demonstrate unconditional love to a greater extent than God. If there is a condition—even one—attached to God's willingness to maintain a relationship with His children, it is not unconditional. On the other hand, I know many people who have demonstrated pure unconditional love to family members who were incredibly undeserving.[4]

Stanley also believes that it would be unreasonable for us to commit ourselves unconditionally to God if He didn't love us unconditionally; that is, if He were only going to commit Himself to us on certain conditions:

> Can we pledge unconditional loyalty to a God who promises only conditional loyalty in return? Isn't it unrealistic to think that we could ever grow comfortable thinking of God as our Dad when we know that if we drift away or fall into sin, the relationship will be severed? ...How deep can my relationship with God really go when He cannot or will not pledge to me His unconditional love and acceptance?[5]

Since God loves us unconditionally, there is no sin or number of sins that would cause God to sever our relationship to Him. Stanley believes that for God to be faithful to the faithless[6] means that no matter how sinful and unbelieving a Christian becomes, he will be kept safe in the Father's hand. "Where sin abounds, grace *super*abounds. Anything less would be less than unconditional."[7] Since God offers us salvation

> **Stanley:**
> Can we pledge unconditional loyalty to a God who promises only conditional loyalty in return?

unconditionally, it would be absurd to think that God would take salvation away for any reason.[8]

God's Holiness

God is holy, which means He is morally perfect. He is set apart from imperfect, sinful man. There is no similarity in the moral goodness of man and God. Because God is so separate from man, a mediator was necessary to bring God and man together. Jesus was willing to bear the sins of man, taking his punishment, so that man could become part of the family of God. God did not compromise His holiness when He let sinful and imperfect man into His family because Christ completely fulfilled for man the requirements of God's holiness. God can tolerate sin in the lives of His children because "God took care of the sin problem once and for all by punishing His Son on our behalf."[9]

Stanley believes that God's holiness is downgraded if man must meet certain conditions to retain his salvation. Assuming that meeting conditions is equivalent to moral effort, Stanley states that when man's moral efforts are inserted into the salvation process, the contrast between God's holiness and man's sinfulness or imperfection is less distinct. Thus God's holiness is depreciated: "To speak of man's moral efforts in conjunction with God's moral perfection is to lessen the contrast and thus downgrade God's holiness."[10] A belief in unconditional eternal security—even (especially?) when it allows for sin to abound in Christians' lives—honors the holiness of God more than a belief in conditional eternal security because *un*conditional eternal security "allows God's holiness to stand in its purest form, free from the feeble attempts to merit divine acceptance."[11]

> **Stanley:**
> God's holiness is downgraded if we must meet conditions to retain salvation.

The nature of God's holiness is not such that it demands something in return from those He loves. If it did, God would be incapable of unconditional love. If one had to be holy to get to heaven, then God's love is not unconditional. But there is nothing in the nature of God that could stand in the way of His ability to love unconditionally. Therefore the holiness of God will not prevent Him from loving His children unconditionally (and keeping them in His family) even when they go astray.[12]

God's Omnipotence

Stanley believes that if something could separate us from the grace of God, that would mean that something is more powerful than God's grace.[13] But God is omnipotent, and there is nothing that can separate Christians from God's unconditional love, not even ourselves.

God's Sovereignty

The purposes of God will not be thwarted, according to Stanley. God "chose us in Him before the foundation of the world," and He has "predestined us to adoption as sons" (Ephesians 1:4,5, NKJ). God would not adopt someone He knew He would eventually have to unadopt. God has purposed that all those who have trusted Christ will go to heaven. If one can lose his place in heaven through sin or unbelief, then "we better cross our fingers and hope Christ ultimately defeats the Antichrist in the end. If mortal man can thwart God's prophetic will for his own life, think of what a supernaturally empowered world leader could do on a universal scale!"[14] If one believes that he can lose his salvation, then he believes that a human being can frustrate the eternal purpose of God. But God has big plans for those whom He has saved, and there is nothing that can stop Him from carrying those plans out. God is sovereign.

Stanley does believe, however, that man still has his freedom. Man is free to reject or choose the gift of salvation. This freedom does not frustrate the purpose of God because God has not purposed that everyone be saved. A distinction needs to be made between the *desires* of God and the *purposes* of God.

> God desires that every person be saved, but He has not purposed that it be so. He has purposed, however, that every person who is saved at any point eventually be the object of His grace in the ages to come. To say that man can do something that causes him to lose his salvation is to say he has the ability to block God in carrying out His purposes. If this is in fact the case, all of prophecy is up for grabs, for how can we legitimately make a distinction between

the purpose of God as stated in Ephesians and that of Revelation?[15]

God knew before the foundation of the world who would choose Him. He wrote their names in the Book of Life before the world began. God would not erase anyone's name from the Book of Life because that would go against both His purpose for all He saves and His foreknowledge.[16]

In summary, God's sovereignty will not be thwarted by man's choices. Though man has the freedom to choose or reject salvation, once he has chosen salvation, he does not have the ability to become unsaved—because God purposes that all whom He ever saves will be the object of His grace throughout eternity.

Wesley's View of Grace and the Nature of God
God's Love

Wesley believed that God graciously loves all mankind. That is why He sent His Son to die for the sins of the whole world and offers to everyone the gift of salvation. This doesn't mean that everyone will be saved; it means that all are given the opportunity to believe in Christ for the salvation from sins. All are loved by God; all who believe are saved (John 3:16). For God to love someone does not mean that they can never be lost; it simply means that God wills everyone's salvation and works to bring everyone to salvation, though He will not violate anyone's free will. "The God of love is willing to save all the souls that He has made. He leaves it up to them."[17]

God exercises a special pardoning love to those who believe in Him. All their past sins are blotted out. Afterwards, God in His love watches over them for good, even as if they had never sinned. However, those who abuse God's love will be disappointed. For if they do not love Him who first loved them, He will gradually and reluctantly withdraw, leaving them in the darkness of their own heart.[18] True believers may lose faith and fall again into condemnation. But as long as they believe and walk after the Spirit, neither God nor their hearts will condemn them (Romans 8:1). Wesley encouraged those who had lost their faith, "Beware thou suffer thy soul to take no rest, till his pardoning love be again revealed; till he heal thy backsliding, and fill thee again with the faith that worketh by love."[19]

Though Wesley believed that one could separate himself from the pardoning love of God, he also believed that God's love is still drawing the backslider to Himself. Wesley told backsliders that God will abundantly pardon them if they return, even if their rebellion was "multiplied as the stars of heaven."[20] God's longsuffering mercy and compassion—His love—is that great.

In summary, though God's love reaches out to the most unlovable, it will only save those who meet the condition of salvation—faith, a faith that must continue. God's love pardons only those who are believing in Christ for salvation from sin. Those who stop believing have removed themselves from God's pardoning love but not from His drawing love—His prevenient grace. If the backslider returns, God's love will abundantly pardon.

God's holiness

For God to be holy means that He is "infinitely distant from every touch of evil."[21] God's holiness cannot tolerate evil. Those He allows into heaven must be "holy as He is holy" (I Peter 1:15-16). Man can and must experience God's sanctifying grace, made available by the blood of Christ, so that his moral nature is changed. "Without holiness no man shall see the Lord" (Hebrews 12:14). This means that "none shall live with God, but he that now lives to God; none shall enjoy the glory of God in heaven, but he that bears the image of God on earth; none that is not saved from sin here can be saved from hell hereafter."[22] For this reason, one must appropriate by faith the sanctifying grace that God offers to every man.

> **Wesley:**
> "None shall live with God, but he that now lives to God."

The God of love is also a holy and just God who punishes the sins that man will not allow Him to forgive. God's love cannot cause God to overlook sin, because God's holiness is as much a part of the essential nature of God as His love. One attribute of God cannot violate another because "all God's attributes are inseparably joined: they cannot be divided, no, not for a moment."[23] God's character will always be consistent. God's love will not override His holiness.[24] Even before a person is saved, he must recognize both the love of God and His holiness:

> By the convicting of the Holy Spirit a man at last sees that the loving, the merciful God is also "a consuming fire," that He is a just God and a terrible, rendering to every man according to his works, entering into judgment with the ungodly for every idle word, yea, and for the imagination of the heart. He now clearly perceives that the great and holy God is "of purer eyes than to behold iniquity;" that He is an avenger of every one who rebelleth against him, and repayeth the wicked to his face, and that "it is a fearful thing to fall into the hands of the living God."[25]

In his Notes on Romans 4:5, Wesley speaks concerning those who have just been saved: "But let none hence presume to continue in sin [after justification]. For to the impenitent God is a consuming fire."[26] One must continue to respect both God's love and His holiness, lest he again face the judgment of God. We should "make full proof of God's mercy, rather than His justice; of His love rather than the thunder of His power."[27] We will experience God's mercy and love, rather than His justice, by exercising true faith in the atoning work of Christ and continuing to trust Him.

In summary, since God is holy and man is a sinner, there is no hope for man to be reconciled to God except as he trusts in Christ as the propitiation for his sin. By His very nature, God cannot overlook unforgiven sin. Those who refuse to appropriate the free grace offered by God on the basis of the merits of His Son, or ultimately reject it even after having experienced it, will face the judgment of a holy and just God.

God's Omnipotence

God is all-powerful. This means that God can do whatever pleases Him.[28] But God's attributes operate in harmony.[29] God's omnipotence cannot overpower His holiness or any other characteristic of God. It will not force salvation on unwilling hearts, since God gave to man His attribute of free will, and He determined from the foundation of the world that those saved will be those who, by God's prevenient grace, voluntarily believe on His

Son and continue to believe on His Son.

God's Sovereignty

God is sovereign over all His creatures and has predetermined from the foundation of the world that by His free grace, those persons who believe and continue to believe will be saved and will walk in holiness.[30] These persons, chosen by God, are called the elect. Wesley here defines the important concept of election:

> Election, in the scripture sense, is God's doing anything that our merit or power have no part in. The true predestination, or foreappointment of God is: 1. He that believeth shall be saved from the guilt and power of sin. 2. He that endureth to the end shall be saved eternally. 3. They who receive the precious gift of faith thereby become the sons of God; and being sons, they shall receive the Spirit of holiness to walk as Christ also walked. Throughout every part of this appointment of God, promise and duty go hand in hand. All is free gift; and yet such is the gift, that the final issue depends on our future obedience to the heavenly call.[31]

God desires that all be saved, but He decreed that He would save those who believe in Christ and continue to believe. God also purposed that those who are saved walk in holiness. "He has predestined us before the foundation of the world that we should be holy" (Eph. 1:4). Those who by God's grace and of their own free will believe and continue to believe to the end will be the ones that God causes to persevere in holiness.

Evaluation

Please see comparison chart, page 31, to better understand the following evaluation.

Charles Stanley has redefined the significance of God's attributes for the Christian's life. Consider what Stanley believes: For God to love His children means that there can be no conditions for salvation after a single act of faith. God's holiness means that there cannot be conditions after salvation, lest His holiness is downgraded. God's omnipotence means that we ourselves do not have the power to reject a relationship with God. Historic Chris-

Grace and the Nature of God	Stanley	Wesley
On God's Love and His Offer of Grace	Since God's love is unconditional for His children, there is nothing they could do to lose their salvation. If one could lose his salvation, we could love unconditionally better than God can.	Though God loves man even when he is unfaithful, salvation and continued salvation is conditioned on faith. God loves the backslider but only reveals His pardoning love to those who continue to express faith in the Son.
On God's Holiness and His Offer of Grace	God's holiness cannot stand in the way of His unconditional love. This means that God will tolerate sin in His children's lives. God's holiness is not violated because Christ paid for all their sin on the cross. To say that sin would separate a Christian from God would be to downgrade holiness, because requiring faithfulness would insert man's moral efforts into the salvation process and make the contrast between man's holiness and God's holiness less distinct.	God's holiness is not superseded by God's love. Though Christ died for everyone's sins on the cross, He did not forgive anyone at the cross; He forgives as one confesses and forsakes his sin. To tolerate persistent sin in the life of a believer would be to downgrade the holiness of God. Because God is holy and just, those who reject His cleansing grace at any time are under condemnation.
On God's Power and His Offer of Grace	God's grace is so powerful that nothing can cause one to lose his salvation.	God's omnipotence will not violate the requirements of His holiness, nor the free will of man. Man can forfeit the saving grace of God if he so chooses.
On God's Sovereignty and His Offer of Grace	God desires that all believe but only the elect will persevere finally in holiness.[32] The elect are those whom God knows from eternity past will at one time or another believe. God purposes that all who ever do believe will be the objects of His grace for eternity.	*Same as Stanley,* though Wesley stressed that the elect would be holy in this life. The elect are those whom God knows from eternity past will believe and continue to believe to the end. All who do so will be the ones whom God causes to persevere in holiness and enjoy the benefits of the grace of God forever.

tianity did not understand God in this way.[33] Stanley overemphasizes the love of God, to the detriment of God's holiness. No doubt Stanley has allowed his belief in unconditional eternal security to shape his understanding of God's nature.

On the other hand Wesley, holding to an orthodox view of God, insists that God's attributes must operate together harmoniously. All the attributes must be kept in balance with one another. The love and holiness of God are to be equally emphasized. The conditional nature of the promises of God cannot be destroyed by an overemphasis on the love of God.

God's power and sovereignty must also be understood in light of everything else that God says about Himself and about the creatures He made in His image. God in his sovereign power does not take away our freedom after we are saved. He has sovereignly decreed that we, as human beings made in the image of God (this image includes freedom and the capacity to be holy), would be given the ability to choose whether or not we would live in a love relationship with God. This ability to choose is not taken away after we are saved. All the warnings in Hebrews confirm that we must persevere in our love relationship with God if we are ultimately to make heaven our home.

Endnotes

1. *Eternal Security*, p. 193.

2. Ibid., 11.

3. Ibid., p. 12.

4. Ibid., pp. 11-12.

5. Ibid., pp. 41-42.

6. "If we are faithless, he remains faithful; for he cannot deny himself" (1 Timothy 2:13).

7. Ibid., p. 193.

8. Ibid.

9. Ibid., p. 103.

10. Ibid.

11. Ibid.

12. Ibid., p. 12.

13. Tape 3, " You Can Be Sure! (Part 1)," *Eternal Security*.

14. *Eternal Security*, p. 42.

15. Ibid., pp. 82-83.

16. Ibid., pp. 180, 182.

17. *Works:* "The Wedding Garment," 7:317.

18. *Works:* "Privilege of Those that are Born of God," 5:233.

19. *Works:* "First Fruits of the Spirit," 5:96.

20. *Works:* "A Call to Backsliders," 6:19.

21. *Works:* "The Unity of the Divine Being," 7:266.

22. *Works:* "A Blow at the Root," 10:364.

23. *Works:* "Predestination Calmly Considered," 10:217.

24. *Works:* "On the Wedding Garment," 7:317. When Wesley teaches in this sermon that true faith cannot supersede holiness, he implies that God's love cannot supersede His holiness.

25. *Works:* "The Spirit of Bondage and Adoption," 5:102.

26. *Notes on the New Testament,* "Romans 4:5."

27. *Works:* "The Great Assize," 5:184.

28. *Works:* "The Unity of the Divine Being," 7:265.

29. *Works:* "On Divine Providence," 6:317-18.

30. John Wesley, *Explanatory Notes on the New Testament* (London: William Bowyer, 1818), "Eph. 1:12."

31. *Explanatory Notes,* "I Peter 1:2."

32. Of course it is one thing to teach that Christians will *ultimately* persevere in faith and holiness, that is, in heaven; it is another thing to teach, with Calvin, that the elect will actually experience growth in faith, and thus holiness, before heaven. Calvin said, "For the Spirit does not merely originate faith, but gradually increases it, until by its means he conducts us into the heavenly kingdom." Calvin's *Institutes,* Book III, chapter 2, section 21.

33. To help show what I mean by Stanley's ideas not being consistent with the historic understanding of the nature of God, I will quote from Thomas Oden's *Systematic Theology,* in which he attempts to present the classical understanding of the relationship between God's holiness and our required response: "God's holiness includes the idea of set-apartness or *separation* from all that is sinful, unworthy of God, or unprepared for God's righteousness. Seen in this way, the holiness to which we are called in response to God's holiness is consecration, or separation from anything that would separate one from God (Gregory Nazianzen, *In Defense of His Flight to Pontus,* NPNF 2 VII, pp. 204 ff.; cf. Teresa of Avila, *Life* CWST, I, pp. 288 ff.). There is profound ethical and political import in the doctrine of God's holiness. God is free from every moral evil; therefore those who are called to holiness of heart and life (Mother Syncletica, 19, SDF, p. 196 cf. Wollebius, CTC XIII, XIV, RD, pp. 75-84; cf. Baxter, PW XV, pp. 539-44; Wesley, WJW VII, pp. 266 ff.) are thereby called to consecrate themselves to a life of radical responsiveness to God's love and accountability to God's own justice." Thomas Oden, *The Living God: Systematic Theology: Volume One,* (New York: HarperCollins, 1987), p. 103. Classical theologians would not say that our attempts to be faithful by God's grace diminishes the holiness of God.

3: ATONEMENT

IS THE EFFECT OF THE ATONEMENT PROVI-
SIONAL OR ABSOLUTE?

The doctrine of atonement may be the doctrine with the most comprehensive implications for Stanley's and Wesley's views of grace and salvation. It is Stanley's view of the atonement which enables him to say that sin does not keep one out of heaven, that faith need only continue for a moment for salvation to be forever, and that "works" have no part to play in salvation. Wesley's view of the atonement causes him to come to much different conclusions.

Stanley on the Atonement

Stanley believes that Jesus Christ, the Lamb of God, took on the sins of the world when He died on the cross. Jesus did not come just to be an example for us or to show us how to live—He came to die for the sins of all mankind.[1] It was necessary for Christ to die on the cross because Christ's substitutionary death was the only act that

Charles Stanley:	John Wesley:
"If the sins you commit after becoming a Christian can annul your relationship with the Savior, clearly those sins were not covered at Calvary."	"Did he then heal the wound before it was made, and put an end to our sins before they had a beginning? This is so glaring, palpable an absurdity, that I cannot conceive how you can swallow it."

could satisfy God's requirement.[2] Man had sinned against a holy God. The penalty of sin was death, physical and spiritual.[3] As a result of his sin, man became separated from God. The only way man could be reconciled to God and escape eternal death was for Christ to pay the penalty of sin for him. Because Christ loved man and wanted him to be reunited with God, He took his place. By suffering death—the punishment originally intended for man—Christ paid the penalty that man had incurred.[4]

This penalty did not just include physical death; it included spiritual death as well.[5] While Jesus was suffering on the cross as our substitute, He became separated from God spiritually.[6] God abandoned Him. During that time, Jesus did not call God Father (as He had previously) but called Him God.[7] The intimate fellowship between Jesus and God was broken. This separation took place in order to pay the price for our sin. Though sin demanded separation from life and separation from God, Christ was willing to pay that penalty in our place. But because Jesus was righteous—He had no sin—He was able to reunite with the Father after a brief period of separation.[8]

Stanley believes that the substitutionary atonement made by Jesus is efficacious for all mankind. The blood of Christ does not have limitations to certain people.[9] The atonement is universal.

Stanley believes in some form of the penal-satisfaction theory of the atonement. He believes that by taking our punishment, Jesus paid the penalty we had incurred. Punishment was suffered for all sins—past, present, and future—once and for all. Since punishment cannot be suffered twice for the same sin, those sins were forever canceled. The atonement is a finished transaction. All who accept the provision of the atonement need never worry that their sins will separate them from God since all their sins—past, present, and future—have been paid for.[10]

At the cross, two things happened. God imputed our sin to Christ, and God imputed Christ's righteousness to us.[11] Scriptural support is in 2 Corinthians 5:21: "He made Him who knew no sin to be sin on our behalf, that we might become the righteousness of God in Him" (NAS). Christ credited us with His righteousness because we must be holy to have fellowship with a holy God.[12] Since God could not ignore sin (and still remain a just God) Christ was credited with our sin. This is why we can be declared by God "not guilty" without God pretending that we are something we are not. We really *are* "not guilty" when we are justified because we have been credited with Christ's righteousness, and He was credited with our sin.[13]

When one is justified, the benefits of the atonement go into effect for that person. The righteousness of Christ is imputed to him—he is made righteous in Christ—and his sin is utterly canceled. But it isn't just his *past* sins that are canceled; *all* his sins are canceled. If one's future sins have not already been forgiven, then the work of the atonement was not completed. Christ would have to come back and die again if one's future sins are not forgiven. But since one's future sins are paid for, there is no way that one could be separated from God for doing them. They were dealt with at the cross.[14]

> ### Stanley:
> Christ would have to come back and die again if our future sins are not forgiven.

Stanley's concept of the atonement is the foundation for his doctrine of eternal security. He argues that since the atonement is a finished work, we cannot lose Christ's payment for our sin. Therefore, God can tolerate sin in the lives of His children after they have been justified. Stanley deals with those that are skeptical of this idea by posing a series of questions:

> Think about it. Which of your sins did Christ take to the cross two thousand years ago? Which of your sins was He punished for? If He died for only part of your sins—for instance, the ones you had committed up to the point of salvation—how can you ever get forgiveness for the sins you commit after that? Would Christ not have to come and die again? And for that matter, again and again and again?
>
> If all your sins were not dealt with on the cross two thousand years ago, there is no hope for you![15]

Stanley emphasizes the objective work of the cross that occurred two thousand years ago. Our sins were covered *then*; they were paid for at the *cross*.[16] This means that the Christian is free from the obligation of paying the penalty for sin. Thus it is impossible for sin to damn the one whose sin is already paid for. This view of the atonement fits perfectly with the concept of unconditional eternal security. Since the debt of sin is paid the believer's salvation is secure.

Wesley on the Atonement

Wesley stated that there is no more important belief than the doctrine of the Atonement. He believed it to be the distinguishing point between Christianity and Deism, a popular religion of his day.[17] According to Wesley, man is truly fallen, and the only way he can be reconciled to God is through the atonement made by Jesus when He died on the cross.

Man needed an atonement because sin had entered into the world and had passed upon all men as a result of the sin of Adam, who was the common father and representative of all mankind.[18] Because of that sin, all men were dead, dead to God, dead in sin, and under the sentence of eternal death. But God, motivated by love, sent His Son to die as a sacrifice for sin so that in the end man might not perish but have everlasting life. Jesus became the second parent and representative of all mankind.[19] As our representative before God, "He bore our griefs... the Lord laying on him the iniquities of us all" (Isaiah 53:4,6). "He bare our sins in His own body on the tree" (I Peter 2:24), becoming a full, perfect, and sufficient sacrifice and satisfaction for the sins of the whole world.[20]

Because of what Jesus did, God has now "reconciled the world to Himself" (II Cor. 5:19). Thus, "as by the offence of one judgment came upon all men to condemnation; even so by the righteousness of one the free gift came upon all men unto justification" (Romans 5:18). Not for the sake of anything that we are or have done or can do, but for the sake of what Jesus did, God now offers us forgiveness of sins and restoration to spiritual life on only one condition—faith (which he also enables us to exercise).[21]

Wesley taught that Jesus died for all men and offers to all men the gift of justification. The following stanza of a poem written by Wesley acknowledges the universality of the atonement:

> *His blood, for all a ransom given,*
> *Has washed away the general sin;*
> *He closed His eyes to open heaven,*
> *And all, who will, may enter in.*[22]

The atonement made the way of salvation open for any person who wants to be saved, not for only a few.

Though Christ died for all, not all men will be saved—because the sacrifice did not *secure* anyone's salvation; it simply provided the basis upon which God could offer salvation on the condition of faith. Christ has done all that is necessary for the *conditional* salvation of all mankind; that is if they believe: "for through his merit all that believe to the end, with the faith that worketh by love, shall be saved."[23]

Wesley did not clearly explicate his own distinctive theory of the atonement, but instead appealed to the traditional Protestant understanding of the atonement. He primarily accepted the penal satisfaction theory, using its language, though he felt that the Calvinists were drawing unbiblical implications from that theory. He also used the language of the ransom theory, the moral influence theory, and the governmental theory, but only insofar as he thought they expressed clear biblical teaching. Wesley considered the atonement a mystery and instead of writing extensively concerning the proper view of the atonement, he stressed the *fact* of the atonement and the way to appropriate its benefits. However, he was concerned (as seen in his writings to Mr. Law) that the atonement be viewed as an objective work whereby the wrath of God towards sinners was appeased and the justice of God satisfied.[24]

> **Wesley:**
> The atonement provides for salvation; it doesn't unconditionally guarantee salvation.

But Wesley was not content with the purely objective view of the atonement that the Calvinists taught. He tried to balance the objective (Christ died once-for-all for the sins of the whole world) with the subjective (that the atonement is only efficacious as individuals personally appropriate its benefits). Actually, Wesley's soteriology does not seem to be totally consistent with his acceptance of the penal satisfaction theory, which usually is perceived as a purely objective view. Where Wesley thought that some of this theory's logical implications did not fit the biblical data, he rejected the implications, instead of rejecting the theory. For instance, Wesley accepted the penal satisfaction idea that Christ was *punished* in man's place. Though

Wesley accepted the idea that Christ was punished instead of man, he refused to accept what that idea might logically imply—that man could never be punished for his sin, since punishment for sin can occur only once.[25] The reason he rejected this implication is that he considered it contrary to the conditional nature of God's promises of salvation and to the very nature of God Himself. To Wesley, the punishment was provisional.

Wesley differed from the penal satisfaction theory when he taught that there is an ongoing application of the atonement that disallows the idea that the benefits of the atonement are automatic or fixed. For Wesley, the atonement was the *foundation* of justification, not the *condition* of justification.[26] He fought against those who would use an idea of the atonement to teach what he thought was a perverted view of imputed righteousness. Many in his day were saying that not only is Christ's passive righteousness (His death) a substitute for our

> **Wesley***:*
> "Oh warn them that if they remain unrighteous, the righteousness of Christ will profit them nothing."

punishment, but also His active righteousness (the righteousness of His life) is a substitute for our life. Accordingly, we do not need to live holy lives because Christ is the substitute for our righteousness. His righteousness has been imputed to us and that is all that matters.[27] Wesley agreed that Christ's righteousness is imputed to those who accept Him,[28] but he stressed that imputed righteousness cannot be different from actual righteousness. For, to whomever Christ imputes righteousness, He also imparts righteousness.[29] In other words, those He counts as righteous, He makes righteous. Furthermore, God will not continue to count as righteous one who refuses to be continually made righteous. Wesley said concerning those who would use the imputed righteousness of Christ as a cover for their unrighteousness: "Oh warn them that if they remain unrighteous, the righteousness of Christ will profit them nothing."[30] The work of the atonement was *not* such that it became unnecessary to be holy. The atonement was not a finished work in the sense that all our future sins were totally destroyed two thousand years ago at the cross and therefore cannot separate us from God.

How did Wesley deal with those he felt drew these unfortunate implications from a purely objective view of the atonement? One way he responded to them was by creating (in an essay) a dialogue between an antinomian[31] and his friend. The friend represents Wesley. Following is an excerpt from the dialogue:

> **Antinomian**: Do you believe...that the "whole work of man's salvation was accomplished by Jesus Christ on the cross?"[32]
> **Friend**: I believe, that, by that one offering, he made a full satisfaction for the sins of the whole world.
> **Antinomian**: But do you believe that "Christ's blood and our sins went away together?"
> **Friend**: To say the truth, I do not understand it.
> **Antinomian**: No! Why, did not Christ, "when he was upon the cross, take away, put an end to, blot out, and utterly destroy, all our sins forever?"
> **Friend**: He did then pay the price, for the sake of which, all who truly believe in him are now saved from their sins; and, if they endure to the end, shall be saved everlastingly. Is this what you mean?
> **Antinomian**: I mean, He did then "heal, take away, put an end to, and utterly destroy, all our sins."
> **Friend**: Did he then heal the wound before it was made, and put an end to our sins before they had a beginning? This is so glaring, palpable an absurdity, that I cannot conceive how you can swallow it.[33]

Wesley did teach that our guilt is imputed to Christ and that His righteousness is imputed to us, but he insisted that this imputation occurs on a conditional basis. When one is justified only *past,* confessed sins are forgiven.[34] Some were saying that the righteousness which justifies us is already carried out, or completed. Wesley called that idea "vain philosophy."[35] The benefits of the atonement are not fixed and automatic. The atonement is objective, but there is a subjective aspect which allows it to be consistent with the character of God. The following quotation from Wesley further illustrates this subjective or experiential aspect of the atonement:

> The sinner being first convinced of his sin and danger by the Spirit of God, stands trembling before the awful tribunal of divine justice; and has nothing to plead but his own guilt and the merits of a Mediator. Christ here interposes. Justice is satisfied: the sin is remitted, and

pardon is applied to the soul, by a divine faith wrought by the Holy Ghost, who then begins the great work of inward sanctification. Thus God justifies the ungodly; and yet remains just and true to all His attributes! But let none hence presume to continue in sin. For to the impenitent God is a consuming fire.[36]

According to Wesley, the moment-by-moment appropriation of the benefits of the atonement by faith is essential for the continuance of those benefits. Though the atonement is a finished work, the high priestly work of Christ is not complete; He daily applies the benefits of the atonement to whom He will. The atonement certainly is the objective satisfaction of the justice of God, but it serves as the *basis* for our justification; it doesn't *guarantee* our justification with no condition. The debt of sin is provisionally paid, not pre-paid. The benefits of the atonement must be continually appropriated by faith. When one sins or fails to fulfill the commands of God perfectly, the blood of Jesus washes him as he confesses his sins and depends on the atonement for cleansing. God does not compromise His holiness when He keeps in His grace a weak Christian who stumbles—because Christ in His continued ministry as intercessor and advocate cleanses with His blood those that confess their sin (I John 1:9) and keeps cleansing those who are walking in the light (I John 1:7), regardless of their infirmities. Christ is faithful to keep under the blood those whom He has redeemed as long as they allow Him to.

Evaluation
Please see comparison chart, pages 42-43, to better understand the following evaluation.

Wesley emphasized both the subjective and objective aspects of the atonement, while Stanley emphasizes the objective. Stanley's emphasis on the objective seems to be at the expense of the ongoing application of the atonement and the actual heart cleansing that occurs when the blood is applied. Stanley thinks that we must appropriate the benefits of the atonement, but for him, what is appropriated is an *imputed* work—righteousness is not necessarily *imparted* to the person appropriating the benefits of the atonement.

Though both debaters correctly view the atonement as necessary

Grace and the Nature of God	Stanley	Wesley
On the Necessity, Motivation, and Extent of the Atonement	The atonement was necessary because of man's sin against a holy God. Love motivated God to send Christ to die for man's sin. Christ's death was a sufficient sacrifice and satisfaction for the sins of the whole world. Jesus died for everyone.	*Same as Stanley*
On the Meaning of the Atonement	Christ was our substitute, who appeased the wrath of God, satisfying the holiness and justice of God when He took our punishment.	*Same as Stanley*
	Emphasis on the objective side of the atonement. Stanley pushes the objective aspect of the penal satisfaction theory to its logical conclusions.	Emphasis on both the objective and subjective. Wesley kept his teaching about the objective side of the atonement in tension with his teachings about its personal application.
On Receiving the Benefits of the Atonement	The benefits of the atonement are conditioned upon our reception of them. But once someone appropriates the benefits of the atonement by faith and is justified, he should look at the atonement as purely objective, with its benefits fixed. All his sins, even future sins, have already been forgiven.	The benefits are conditional upon our *continual* reception of them. Christians should not look at the atonement as purely objective. The benefits of the atonement are always provisional. One is only cleansed from his sins as he trusts in the blood. The atonement does not forgive sins before they are committed; rather, the atonement provides for forgiveness, and the blood is actually applied to cleanse one's sins when he confesses them, at the time of regeneration or later.
On the Penalty Christ Paid for Us	Since the penalty of death includes both physical and spiritual death, Christ died both physically and spiritually.	Christ as our substitute paid our penalty of death, though Christ did not die spiritually.
On Substitution and Imputation	Christ was the substitute for our punishment and for our righteousness.	Christ was the substitute for our punishment.

Continued...

Grace and the Nature of God	Stanley	Wesley
Substitution and Imputation	The imputation of Christ's righteousness is a constant and does not always accompany the impartation of His righteousness.	Christ's righteousness was imputed to us, but imputation always coincides with the reality of things so that one is always made or kept *actually* righteous if he is *counted* as righteous.
On Whether Sins were Canceled at the Cross.	All our sins—past, present, and future—were paid for at the cross. They were blotted out, canceled, at the cross.	Sins must be committed before they can be blotted out. Christ didn't cancel out all sin at the cross; He simply paid the price, for the sake of which, all who truly believe in Him are *now* saved from their sins; and, if they endure to the end, shall be forever saved.

and substitutional, Stanley unsuccessfully tries to wed the Calvinistic penal substitution theory with the Arminian teaching that Jesus died for all.[37] He cannot have it both ways. If the Calvinistic view of the atonement is correct (our sins were done-away-with at the cross), then either limited atonement or universalism is true.

Stanley teaches that all sins were canceled—blotted out—at the cross. One might ask him why faith is not superfluous if all our sins were dealt with fully at the cross. How could anyone be punished for his sins if Christ took everyone's punishment in the sense that Stanley teaches?

Wesley taught that Christ's payment for sin provided the way for man to be forgiven of his sins when he confesses them. Stanley, taking the effect of the atonement much further, teaches that the atonement paid for sins in such a way that if one accepts this payment, then not only are all past sins forgiven, but also all future sins are forgiven in advance. If the atonement paid for sins in this absolute sense, the doctrine of unconditional eternal security stands; if it doesn't, then the doctrine of unconditional eternal security comes crashing down. But this view of the atonement is suspect. Stanley needs to be asked: When was my sin forgiven, at the cross or when I received Christ? If my sins were forgiven at the cross, then either Christ atoned for only the elect, or everyone is forgiven and will go to heaven. If my sins were forgiven when I received Christ, it is because forgiveness was only *provided for* at the cross. The atonement is provisional, not absolute. No one can claim to be forgiven for sins not yet committed, just as no one can claim to have his clothes washed from future dirt. We are cleansed of past sins by "plunging into the cleansing stream," the Holy Spirit applying the atoning work of Christ to our own hearts. When we confess our sins, the blood of Jesus Christ cleanses us from the stain of those sins (I John 1:9). The very nature of this "cleansing" action suggests that the application is personal and ongoing, occurring as we trust in the atoning sacrifice.

John Wesley was right when he taught that the benefits of the atonement are conditioned on our continued reception of them. The atonement *provides* salvation; it does not *guarantee* salvation with no condition. Wesley was also right to challenge what turned out to be Stanley's extreme view of imputed righteousness. Christ's righteousness is imputed to us only when (but not after) it is imparted to us. We cannot hide our unrighteousness under the cloak of the righteousness of Christ.

Endnotes

1. Tape one, "Where It All Begins," *Eternal Security.*

2. Ibid.

3. *Eternal Security,* p. 32.

4. Ibid., p. 31.

5. Ibid., p. 32.

6. Ibid., pp. 31, 32.

7. Ibid., p. 32.

8. Stanley teaches that Christ's sinlessness not only enabled him to be reconciled to His Father but also made Him the only acceptable sacrifice for sin. Ibid., p. 32.

9. Tape 1, "Where It All Begins," *Eternal Security.*

10. *Eternal Security,* pp. 34, 35.

11. Ibid., p. 31.

12. Ibid., p. 29.

13. Ibid., pp. 30, 31.

14. Ibid., p. 35.

15. Ibid., p. 34.

16. If one's sins were covered at Calvary, they were covered *before* one trusted Christ. That is why Stanley can say that sin will not keep us out of heaven; only unbelief will.

17. John Telford, ed. *The Letters of the Rev. John Wesley, A. M.* (London: The Epworth Press, 1931), 6:297.

18. *Works:* "Justification by Faith," 5:55.

19. Ibid.

20. Ibid.

21. Ibid., p. 239.

22. G. Osborne, collector, *The Poetical Works of John and Charles Wesley, 13 vols.* (London: Wesleyan-Methodist Conference Office, 1868-72), "Free Grace," 3:93.

23. *Works:* "An Extract from 'A Short View of the Difference Between the Moravian Brethren (so called), and the Rev. Mr. John and Charles Wesley,'" 10:202.

24. *Works:* "Extract of a Letter to the Rev. Mr. Law," 9:480-493.

25. He tries to avoid this implication by saying that sin can't be punished before it is committed. Neither can sin be forgiven before it is committed. "Whatever punishment he redeems us from, that punishment supposes sin to precede: which must exist first, before there is any possibility of it being either punished or pardoned." *Works:* "A Second Dialogue Between an Antinomian and His Friend," 10:279. Wesley is arguing for the subjective aspect of the work of the atonement. Christ's work as mediator between God and man is ongoing though the sacrifice was once-for-all. (Wesley soundly rejects the repeated sacrifice of the sacraments of the Roman Catholics.)

26. *Works:* "Preface to A Treatise on Justification," 10:322.

27. Wesley accepted the idea that Jesus was our substitute as to penal sufferings but he argued against the idea that Christ's obedience was the substitute for our obedience (in the sense that God doesn't see our unrighteousness but only Jesus' righteousness). Ibid., p. 319.

28. In fact, Wesley said that the human righteousness of Christ, at least the imputation of it, is "the whole and sole meritorious cause of the justification of a sinner before God." *Works:* "The Lord Our Righteousness," 5:242. Justification was given to no one for the sake of what they were or could do, but "wholly and solely for the sake of what Christ hath done and suffered for them." Ibid., p. 239. For Wesley, inherent righteousness is not the basis for our acceptance with God; however, it is always the fruit of it. In other words, to whomever Christ imputes righteousness, he also imparts righteousness. Ibid., p. 241.

29. Ibid.

30. Ibid., p. 244. For Wesley, the inward state of the heart is never different from the way God sees man. If one refuses to let God change him on the inside, he cannot expect to be counted righteous by God.

31. An antinomian is someone who thinks that Christ, having fulfilled the law for him, has eliminated the necessity of righteous living. Wesley had to deal with both active and passive antinomianism. Active antinomianism encouraged lawlessness while passive antinomianism allowed it.

32. The phrases in quotation marks are from the teachings of some of those Wesley considered antinomian.

33. *Works:* "A Dialogue between an Antinomian and His Friend," 10:267.

34. *Works:* "Justification by Faith," 5:57. To say that Christ only forgives confessed sins does not mean that one has to remember every sin he has ever committed. It means that we must admit that we have sinned and that we repudiate our rebellion in general and any specific sin that God brings to our attention. We must by faith keep close to the atoning

sacrifice to receive His forgiveness whenever we need it.

35. *Works:* "A Preface to A Treatise on Justification," 10:319.

36. *Notes on the New Testament:* "Romans 4:5."

37. While a Calvinist might argue that some of Christ's blood is "wasted" if not everyone for whom Christ died is saved, both Stanley and Wesley would affirm that Christ died for sins that will never, in practice, be forgiven (since both views affirm universal atonement, deny universal salvation, and require a human response). To both Stanley and Wesley, the atonement is conditional. Therefore, from a Calvinistic perspective, Stanley's assertion that it takes a moment of faith to apply Christ's atonement has no advantage over Wesley's that it takes continuous faith as far as the sufficiency of Christ's death is concerned.

4: STANLEY'S *ORDO SALUTIS*

WHAT ARE THE CONDITIONS FOR SALVATION?

Having looked at Wesley's and Stanley's view of the atonement, we now turn in the next two chapters to the "order of salvation." Prevenient grace, repentance, saving faith, justification, regeneration, assurance, and sanctification will be the subjects of discussion. Because of length, this chapter will cover Stanley's order of salvation, and chapter five will cover Wesley's order of salvation. At the end of that chapter, the two will be compared and contrasted.

Stanley's Order of Salvation

Stanley believes that salvation is at its core a removal of guilt from sin.[1] Since the removal of the guilt of sin means deliverance from the consequence of sin—eternal death—Stanley can define sal-

Charles Stanley:	John Wesley:
"If I chose to have a tattoo put on my arm, that would involve a one-time act on my part. Yet the tattoo would remain with me indefinitely…. [Likewise] salvation is applied at the moment of faith. It is not the same thing as faith. And its permanence is not contingent upon the permanence of one's faith."	"Without faith, notwithstanding all our present holiness, we should be devils the next moment. But as long as we retain our faith in him, we draw waters out of the wells of salvation."

vation as deliverance from eternal death and possession of eternal life.[2] Stanley limits salvation to this definition to prevent misunderstandings concerning how one is saved and kept saved. The significance of the definition will become clearer as the reader proceeds through the following presentation of Stanley's *ordo salutis*.

Prevenient Grace

Though Stanley's books make no reference to prevenient grace, a short presentation of his idea of grace in general might be useful here. Stanley believes that God's grace is responsible for man's salvation from start to finish:

> Grace encapsulates the entire salvation process. It encapsulates the sending of Christ, the offer of forgiveness, His crucifixion, His resurrection, and His ascension. Why grace? Because grace indicates unmerited favor; it suggests an undeserved expression of kindness and goodwill. The whole of salvation is just that—an undeserved gift. From start to finish, salvation is by grace… How did God save us?…By grace; by an undeserved series of events enacted for our benefit.[3]

Stanley sees grace as those undeserved kindnesses that God has done, is doing, and will do for our salvific benefit. Grace covers the whole salvation process.

To Stanley, God's grace is what moved Him to sacrifice His Son to provide a way for our salvation. By grace, the way of salvation is offered to all. God's offer of grace is continually extended to even the most vile sinner.[5] His grace knows no limits, either in breadth or in duration.[6]

It seems that Stanley does not see grace as an enabling power, but simply as unmerited favor. This may be the reason that no discussion was found in Stanley's writings concerning the doctrine of prevenient grace. In historic Christian thought, prevenient grace went before salvation, working in hearts to produce desires for spiritual things.[7] In Stanley's view, God's grace before salvation seems to be limited to an offer of forgiveness (based on Christ's objective work).

Repentance

In Stanley's order of salvation, repentance follows God's offer of salvation and precedes faith. In his view, there are two kinds of repentance, both of which mean basically a "change of mind." The first repentance occurs before salvation and is a change of mind about Christ—who He is and what He has done for us.[8] The second repentance occurs after salvation and is a change of mind about behavior; a repenting for sins.[9] The first repentance, which is necessary for salvation, has nothing to do with changing one's behavior or turning from one's sins; it is simply a change of mind about Christ.[10] It is necessary for salvation only because one cannot trust Christ for salvation until he has changed his thinking to a basic understanding of who Christ is and what He did.

The second repentance, which occurs after salvation, is the only repentance that deals with sin. This repentance is very important in the life of the believer; it is vital to one's fellowship with Christ. However, it is not necessary for the gaining or the maintaining of one's salvation.[11]

> **Stanley:**
> Repentance for salvation has nothing to do with turning from one's sins.

To Stanley, it is imperative for one to realize that repentance before salvation is not a change of mind about behavior, for if one believes that he was saved partly by getting his life straightened up, he will think that he must *maintain* his salvation by keeping his life straightened up. But it is impossible for one to become saved or stay saved by changing his behavior. Changing one's lifestyle will not do any good; it will not make one acceptable to God. Repentance of sin is not the biblical method of getting saved—faith is. Stanley argues that a change in behavior will not save anyone because man's problem is deeper than that—man's problem is his corrupted nature.[12]

To show that repentance from sin is not necessary for *keeping* one's salvation, Stanley uses the prodigal son as a biblical illustration of someone who did not need to repent to be restored to his father's favor. (The father is a picture of the Heavenly Father.) "The father demanded no explanation; no apology; nothing. There was no probationary period, just acceptance and joy."[13] Since the son was always the son, his rebellion had only broken fellowship with the father, not the relationship. Repentance was not needed to restore the relationship; it was always intact. And repentance was not necessary to restore fellowship either; there is no indication that the father expected any contrition or restitution. The father took immediate action to restore his son to a place of honor and dignity. Repentance was not necessary because the father's love and acceptance was not contingent on the son's works.[14] To require repentance from sin as a requirement for salvation or restoration to salvation would be to teach salvation by works, not grace.[15]

Saving Faith

In Stanley's order of salvation, repentance is followed by faith. Saving faith, though necessarily preceded by repentance (a change of mind about Christ), is the only condition for salvation.[16]

Stanley believes that saving faith is faith in Christ, but he believes that it is more than just believing who Christ is or believing what He did.[17] It is *trusting* in Him as Savior: "If I truly believe for salvation, I place my trust in Him as God's only begotten Son who paid my sin debt on the cross of Calvary for all my sin and do receive Him as my personal Savior."[18] To put it another way, "Faith is the means by which the saving work of Christ is applied to the individual. Specifically, salvation comes to the individual when that person places trust in Christ's death on the cross as the complete payment for sin."[19]

Trust is more than belief; it is a confident dependence and a commitment. It is walking out onto a bridge rather than simply believing that the bridge will hold you up. Trust denotes personal involvement.[20]

Stanley teaches something else about the nature of saving faith when he makes it clear that, since grace is what saves us, we are not saved *by* faith; we are saved *through* faith. Stanley says that the term "through" is the key to understanding the significance of faith. "Through" is translated from the Greek word *dia*, which conveys the idea of "means" or "agency".[21] Faith is the agent by which God applies His grace to the life of the sinner, or that which "bridges the gap between our need and God's provision."[22] Faith doesn't save us; it just brings God's provision together with our need. A lady who jumps from a burning building into the safety net of firefighters does not save herself by her leap. Her leap of faith (faith in the firefighters) doesn't save her; the firefighters' net does. Her leap of faith simply brings the provision of the net together with her need. When one expresses saving faith, he brings God's provision together with his need. Once the woman jumps, she is saved. Once one believes in Christ, he is saved. And just as the lady has no more danger of facing the fire of that burning building, a saved person has no more danger of facing the fires of eternal damnation.[23]

The illustration just mentioned brings this discussion to what Stanley would consider a very important question concerning the nature of saving faith: How long must saving faith endure for salvation to be permanent? Stanley goes to great lengths in *Eternal Security*—especially in chapters eight and nine: "For Those Who Stop Believing" and "He Who Believes..."—to make a case that saving faith need only be of a moment's duration for one's salvation to be forever secure. The relationship between faith and salvation is such that a moment of trust is all that is necessary for permanent salvation. Stanley supports this view by arguing that salvation and faith are entities that can exist independently of one another:

> Faith is simply the way we say yes to God's free gift of eternal life. Faith and salvation are not one and the same anymore than a gift and the hand that receives it are the same. Salvation or justification or adoption—whatever you wish to call it—stands independently of faith. Consequently, God does not require a *constant attitude* of faith in order to be saved—only an *act* of faith.
>
> [An] illustration may be helpful. If I chose to have a tattoo put on my arm, that would involve a one-time act on my part. Yet the tattoo would remain with me indefinitely. In fact, I may change my mind the minute I receive it. But that does not change the fact that I have a tattoo on my arm. My request for the tattoo and the tattoo itself are two entirely different things. I received it by asking and paying for it. But asking for my money back and changing my attitude will not undo what is done.
>
> Forgiveness/salvation is applied at the moment of faith. It is not the same thing as faith. And its permanence is not contingent upon the permanence of one's faith.[24]

Stanley here explicates his understanding of the nature of true saving faith and the nature of salvation itself. To him, salvation is a static state. It exists independently of faith. The relationship between faith and salvation is such that the one (salvation) can exist without the other (faith). This means that even if faith totally disintegrates, salvation will still survive as a once-for-all gift to the one receiving it by the one-time act of faith.

> **Stanley:**
> Once salvation is secured by an act of faith, faith is no longer necessary for salvation.

Stanley is not saying that one can be saved without faith, but he is saying that faith need only continue but for a moment. Once the gift of salvation is secured by an act of faith, faith is no longer necessary for salvation.

Another way Stanley argues against the necessity of continued faith for salvation is to appeal to the metaphor Paul used in Ephesians 2:8 to describe salvation: it is a gift. To place conditions on the permanency of salvation is to say it is not a gift. To Stanley, a gift is not a gift if it can be taken back or if there are any strings attached. Once someone places a condition of any kind on a gift, it becomes a trade, not a gift. If one does try to give the gift back, the Giver, in the case of salvation, will not accept the return. God has a strict no-return policy.[25] Stanley claims that there is no evidence by way of statement or illustration that God has ever taken back from a believer the gift of salvation once it has been given.[26] Since salvation is a gift that cannot be taken back, faith, as the spiritual hand that receives the gift, need only be extended for a moment of time.[27] One does *not* need to continue to believe in order to retain possession of the gift of salvation.

Stanley argues against those who say that the use of the *present* tense for "believe" in verses like "whoever believes in him shall have eternal life" means that one must *continuously* believe in order to continue to be saved. He thinks that this argument is erroneous. He contends that the normal use of the present tense does not denote continuous, uninterrupted action.[28] If he says to someone, "I live in Atlanta," he doesn't mean that he is continuously there—that he never goes out of town. The Bible as well, being consistent with our normal usage, rarely uses the present tense to denote uninterrupted, continuous action.[29] For instance, when Jesus met the Samaritan women at the well, He told her, "Those who *drink* from this well will thirst again..." *Drink* is in the present tense. But it would be a physical impossibility for someone to drink continuously at the Samaritan well. Besides, if they did drink continuously, they would not ever thirst again, contrary to what Jesus said.[30] Therefore, the present tense should not usually be taken to mean continuous action. Since this is the case, verses which use the present tense form of "believe" in relation to salvation do not mean that one must continuously believe in order to continue to be saved.

Two of his quotations summarize Stanley's view of saving faith: "You and I are not saved because we have enduring faith. We are saved because at a moment in time we expressed faith in our enduring Lord."[31] Or to express the concept in another way: "Saving faith is not necessarily a sustained attitude of gratefulness for God's gift. It is a singular moment in time wherein we take what God has offered."[32]

Justification

Stanley believes that when one truly exercises saving faith in Christ, he is justified.[33] To be justified is to be declared "not guilty."[34] The reason people can be declared not guilty when they were guilty is *not* because God pretends they are not guilty.[35] The reason is the atonement.

For Stanley, justification (declaration of "not guilty") is not an end in itself; it is the means to an end.[36] When God justifies people, he forgives them and adopts them into his family. He justifies people in order to restore a personal relationship with them.[37] Once a person has been adopted into God's family, that relationship can never be changed. The Father would never become a Judge again and declare a person "guilty" after declaring him "not guilty":

> The good news is that after the Judge pronounced you and me "not guilty," He walked from behind the bench and welcomed us into His family. The days of the courtroom are over... As a believer, you will never be judged for your sins. It is so settled in the mind of God that at the moment of your salvation, knowing full and well all the sins you were yet to commit, God adopted you into His family.[38]

Regeneration

Stanley refers very little to regeneration, a major concomitant of justification. Justification, forgiveness, and adoption are important to Stanley's work *Eternal Security*, but he is silent on regeneration, other than referring to himself as being born again (with no explanation). There is not much evidence that Stanley believes that one experiences a real heart change when he is saved. In his book *The Wonderful Spirit-filled Life*, he does say that when one is saved he is set free from the bondage of sin, but he qualifies the statement:

> When we trusted Christ as our Savior, we were placed into Christ. At that point in time we were set free from slavery to sin (see Rom. 6:22). The leash was cut. We no longer had to give in to the temptations of Satan or the desires of our sinful flesh. But nobody told us! So when a temptation came along, what did we do? What we had always done— we gave in. But we felt guilty because the Holy Spirit was living in us. And he was grieved.[39]

If Stanley is talking about an inward renewal of the heart, this renewal does not necessarily result in changed behavior.

On Stanley's sermon tapes there are allusions to a heart change that occurs after justification, but clarity on the subject is greatly lacking. He seems to suggest that the norm for a Christian life is that one's desires will begin to change when he is saved; one will begin to repent of his sins and turn from them, and he will begin to desire spiritual things. Stanley feels that this is very important in the life of a believer.[40]

Assurance

Stanley believes the privilege of every believer is that he can know that he is saved:

> John wrote an entire epistle to assure a group of people...that they were in fact saved: "These things I have written to you who believe in the name of the Son of God, in order that you may know that you have eternal life."[41]

For Stanley, assurance of salvation is closely associated with the doctrine of eternal security. He writes, "If you and I have any part in the maintaining our salvation, it will be difficult to live with much assurance. Hope, yes; assurance, no."[42]

Assurance rests on the understanding and acceptance of the doctrine of eternal security—that our security rests in the hands of an unconditionally loving Heavenly Father.[43] Stanley says that this doctrine is supported with verses like Romans 8:37-39, which teaches that nothing can separate the Christian from the love of God.[44]

Belief in eternal security is not the only ingredient of assurance, however. From *The Wonderful Spirit-filled Life*, it is evident that Stanley considers the presence of the Holy Spirit the source of assurance. "We know that we belong to Christ because His Spirit dwells in us. Without Him, there is no assurance."[45]

> **Stanley:**
> Once a person has been adopted into God's family, that relationship can never be changed.

Stanley believes that if one does not have assurance of salvation, his Christian life will be hindered. Stanley describes (in his book on eternal security) the years he lived as a young man under fear and guilt wondering if he were in or out of grace. He had been saved in a Pentecostal Holiness Church that taught that if you sinned, you would lose your salvation. As a boy, he found himself continually confessing his sins hoping he wouldn't die before he had time to repent. (It seemed that everything that was fun to a boy was sin to the church.) Stanley describes how he felt after he got a call to the ministry as a teenager: "The awareness of God's call in my life only darkened the cloud of guilt under which I lived. *How could I ever help anybody else when I'm constantly wavering?* I would wonder. *What if I stood to preach and wasn't even saved?*"[46] Though he never felt lost during the ups and downs of his early Christian life (instead of feeling alienated from God during his lowest times, he always felt His peace),[47] he was only truly delivered from his guilt and fears when he accepted the doctrine of eternal security, and thus became settled in the assurance of his salvation.

Stanley felt that, without this kind of assurance, one could not fully experience the fruit of the Spirit:

> Where there is no assurance of God's acceptance, there is no peace. Where there is no peace, there is no joy. Where there is no joy, there

is a limitation on one's ability to love unconditionally. Why? Because a person with no assurance is by definition partially motivated by fear. Fear and love do not mingle well. One will always dilute the other. Furthermore, fear spills over into worry. Let's be realistic for a moment. If my salvation is not a settled issue, how can I be anxious for nothing (see Phil. 4:6)?[48]

This assurance of salvation can only be a settled issue if one believes in eternal security. "I know from experience that until you settle once and for all the question of whether or not you are eternally secure, this quality of joy will elude you."[49]

Sanctification

Stanley believes that Christians were sanctified or made holy through the death of Christ.[50] The phrase "we have been sanctified" in Hebrews 10:10 means that believers have been made holy; set apart; cleansed to the point of enabling them to enter into relationship with a holy God.[51] This sanctifying is something that occurred once—at the cross. "Have been sanctified" is a verb whose tense denotes a one-time action with continuing results.[52] Hebrews 10:12 spells out the reason it is a once-for-all operation—Christ's death was "one sacrifice for all time."[53] One can conclude that sanctification is something that has already taken place objectively at the cross and cannot happen again; therefore, there is no danger of losing the benefit of that sanctification once one has received it.[54]

This sanctification seems to be something that affects one's legal standing before God, but not something that actually occurs in the heart of the believer. Whatever else this sanctification does for the believer, it does not deal with the flesh—the sinful nature. Stanley confesses that the "flesh" is not something that can be improved or eliminated,[55] though in the objective sense it has been nailed to the cross.

> **Stanley:**
> Sanctification already happened at the cross; therefore Christians are in no danger of losing it.

Those who have become Christians have been set free from the bondage of the flesh—they don't have to yield to its desires, but they will still have to battle it.[56]

Stanley believes that the only way that one can get the victory over the flesh and sin is through the Spirit-filled life.[57] The Spirit-filled life will not deliver a person from the presence of the sinful flesh but will give him power over it.[58] In *The Wonderful Spirit-filled Life,* Stanley tells his own experience of entering into the Spirit-filled life and shows Christians how they can experience it as well.

Stanley describes the wonderful Spirit-filled life to those Christians living defeated lives who want victory. He explains that though all Christians are indwelt by the Spirit and filled by the Spirit,[59] there is a sense in which one is filled with the Spirit after he is saved (in the case of Ephesians 5:18—"Be filled with the Spirit").[60] To be filled with the Spirit in this sense is to "voluntarily put oneself under the influence of the Holy Spirit."[61] The Spirit-filled life is a life of working in harmony with the Holy Spirit.[62] It is walking in the Spirit.[63] Walking in the Spirit can be defined as living with moment-by-moment dependency on and sensitivity to the initial promptings of the Holy Spirit.[64] Walking in the Spirit will produce the fruit of the Spirit and give victory over sin.

Walking in the Spirit (living the Spirit-filled life) is something that not all Christians do, but it is a life that all Christians can experience if they meet the conditions.[65] One can experience this wonderful Spirit-filled life by first recognizing that there is such a life, that he can experience it, and that the Spirit who indwells him has the power and desire to bring about great change in his character and perspective.[66] When these truths become part of one's thinking, he will be transformed.

Another necessary truth one must recognize is that he is free from sin. If a person doesn't recognize this fact, he will assume that the tug of the flesh is a tug he cannot resist. "You may feel the way you have always felt. You may desire the things you have always desired. But the fact is, you are free. Begin now renewing your mind to this transformational truth, for you will never walk in the Spirit until you are convinced of your freedom."[67]

As stated before, Stanley believes Christians are potentially set free from the bondage of sin when they are saved. But the Christian may not actually quit sinning until he realizes he *can* quit sinning through the indwelling Holy Spirit, who is willing and able to empower him.

The Christian desiring a Spirit-filled life must also come to the place of total dependence and total surrender.[68] "The Spirit-filled life begins once we are absolutely convinced that we can do nothing apart from the indwelling strength of the Holy Spirit."[69] When a Christian recognizes the victory that he has through the Holy Spirit and yields himself to His control, he will begin to live the Spirit-filled life.

The Spirit-filled life is a life of faith. It started by faith, and it continues by faith. Stanley believes that the Bible does not make a distinction between the faith that saves Christians from the penalty of sin once and the faith that saves them from the power of sin daily.[70] The Christian must continue to exercise faith in Christ to maintain victory over sin (though not to maintain salvation).

Since the Spirit-filled life is a life of faith, a believer's efforts have no part in the production of Christian fruit. Stanley says that for a time he tried to live the Christian life by "works" and found that his efforts were fruitless:

> For some strange reason, after entering into this wonderful relationship [salvation] by faith, I began conducting it by works. It was as if I said to God, "Thanks for the gift. I'll take it from here." I wrongly assumed that it was my responsibility to produce righteousness, that God had left it up to me to change myself and become a better person.
>
> How absurd! If I could produce righteousness on my own, why did Christ need to die for me? The truth is, on my own I can't produce one ounce of righteousness, neither before nor after salvation. As believers, our potential for righteous living is in direct proportion to our willingness to allow the Holy Spirit to produce His fruit through us.[71]

In fact, one should not even concentrate on fruit-bearing. He should commit himself to walk in the Spirit. The result of that commitment will be the fruit of the Spirit.[72] Stanley says, "Remember, fruit is not something you produce; it's something that takes you by surprise as the Holy Spirit produces it through you."[73] He explains why it is futile to try to produce fruit ourselves:

> Trying to produce righteousness ourselves is like trying to grow apples on a grapevine...Our unredeemed, selfish, sinful flesh is not tooled to produce good fruit...When we take the responsibility of producing

the fruit of the Spirit ourselves, we are attempting to improve our flesh…[But] My flesh has not improved one bit.[74]

What is a Spirit-filled person like? The mark of a Spirit-filled Christian is the fruit that he bears. Fruit (not gifts or talents) is the standard by which the Christian's walk can be measured.[75] The immediate result of walking by the Spirit is that a person will not carry out the desires of the flesh. Stanley says, "Saying no to the desires of the flesh will be the natural outcome of walking in the Spirit."[76] The person walking by the Spirit, and thus being led by the Spirit, will bear the fruit of the Spirit instead.

In summary, though Stanley does not believe that there is a work of God that can actually cleanse the Christian in this life of the "sinful flesh"—sanctification is an imputed work—he does teach a deeper commitment to God that results

> **Stanley:**
> "Saying no to the desires of the flesh will be the natural outcome of walking in the Spirit."

in a life of victory over known sin and a life of fruitful service. This life of victory is termed the wonderful Spirit-filled life.

Endnotes

1. *Eternal Security*, p. 30.
2. Tape 1, "Where it All Begins," *Eternal Security*.
3. *Eternal Security*, p. 75.
4. Ibid., p. 118.
5. Ibid.
6. Ibid., p. 9, 76, 77.
7. The Second Council of Orange (A. D. 529) states: "The sin of the first man has so impaired and weakened free will that no one thereafter can either love God as he ought or believe in God or do good for God's sake, unless the grace of divine mercy has preceded him."
8. Tape 1, "Where it All Begins," *Eternal Security*.
9. Tape 2, "Does it Really Matter," *Eternal Security*.
10. Tape 1, "Where it All Begins," *Eternal Security*.
11. Tape 2, "Does it Really Matter," *Eternal Security*.
12. Ibid.
13. *Eternal Security*, p. 53.
14. Ibid., p. 53.
15. Ibid., pp. 46, 49, 53.

16. Ibid., pp. 67, 71.

17. Tape 1, "Where it All Begins," *Eternal Security.*

18. Ibid.

19. *Eternal Security,* p. 32.

20. Ibid., pp. 69, 70.

21. Ibid., p. 78.

22. Ibid., p. 79.

23. Ibid., pp. 79, 80.

24. Ibid., p. 80.

25. Ibid., p. 81.

26. Ibid.

27. Ibid.

28. Ibid., p. 85.

29. Ibid., p. 86.

30. Ibid.

31. Ibid., p.80

32. Ibid., p. 81.

33. Ibid., p. 37.

34. Ibid., p. 30.

35. Ibid.

36. Ibid., p. 39.

37. Ibid.

38. Ibid.

39. Charles Stanley, *The Wonderful Spirit-filled Life* (Nashville: Thomas Nelson Publishers, 1992), p. 90.

40. Tape 1, "Where it All Begins," *Eternal Security.*

41. *Eternal Security,* p. 9. Stanley is quoting 1 John 5:13.

42. Ibid., p. 9.

43. Ibid., p. 192.

44. Ibid., pp. 141, 142.

45. *The Wonderful Spirit-filled Life,* pp. 86, 87.

46. *Eternal Security,* p. 2.

47. Ibid., p. 3.

48. Ibid., pp. 9, 10.

49. Ibid., p. 5.

50. Ibid., p. 52.

51. Ibid.

52. Ibid., p. 152.

53. Ibid., pp. 52, 54.

54. Ibid., p. 152.

55. *The Wonderful Spirit-filled Life*, p. 75.

56. Ibid., p. 111.

57. Ibid., p. 65.

58. Ibid., pp. 75, 90.

59. Stanley believes that *all* Christians are filled with the Spirit in a sense. He says that the apostles Paul and John both believed that believers everywhere were filled with the Spirit. Once a person has trusted Christ as Savior, he has been baptized by the Spirit, he is indwelt, and he is filled. He therefore has everything he needs to experience the wonderful Spirit-filled life. But he might be living below his privileges and might need an experience with God through faith that will enable him to experience life in the Spirit. *The Wonderful Spirit-filled Life*, pp. 96, 162.

60. Ibid., p. 45.

61. Ibid.

62. Ibid., p. 83.

63. Throughout the book *The Wonderful Spirit-filled Life*, Stanley seems to use the terms *Spirit-filled life* and *walking in the Spirit* somewhat interchangeably.

64. Ibid., p. 88.

65. Ibid.

66. Ibid., p. 71.

67. Ibid., pp. 90-91.

68. Ibid., p. 47.

69. Ibid.

70. Ibid., p. 76.

71. Ibid., p. 72.

72. Ibid., p. 102.

73. Ibid., p. 103.

74. Ibid., p. 75.

75. Ibid., pp. 107, 136.

76. Ibid., p. 89.

5: WESLEY'S *ORDO SALUTIS*

A t the end of this chapter, after having discussed Wesley's order of salvation, we will compare it to Stanley's order of salvation, which was treated in the previous chapter.

Wesley's Order of Salvation

Wesley defined salvation as a present salvation (obtainable on earth) from sin (from original and actual sin, and from past and present sin). It is salvation from the guilt, the power, and the consequences of sin. Since it is a salvation from guilt, it is also salvation from the *fear* of punishment and the *fear* of falling away from the grace of God (though not a salvation from the *possibility* of falling).[1] Wesley also included both justification and sanctification (including entire sanctification) in his description of salvation.[2] In a broad sense, salvation includes even prevenient grace.[3] Wesley said that salvation might be extended "to the entire work of God, from the first dawning of grace in the soul, till

---

Charles Stanley:	John Wesley:
We really are "not guilty" when we are justified because we have been credited with Christ's righteousness, and He was credited with our sin.	When God justifies someone, He does not deceive himself into thinking that something is other than what really is; that He considers someone righteous who is not. God imparts righteous to anyone He imputes righteousness.

---

it is consummated in glory."[4] The following sections will expand the successive stages of salvation that Wesley summarizes here:

> Salvation begins with what is usually termed (and very properly) *preventing grace*: including the first wish to please God, the first dawn of light concerning his will, and the first slight transient conviction of having sinned against him. All these imply some tendency toward life; some degree of salvation; the beginning of a deliverance from a blind, unfeeling heart…Salvation is carried on by *convincing grace*, usually in Scripture termed *repentance*; which brings a large measure of self-knowledge and a further deliverance from a heart of stone. Afterwards we experience the proper Christian salvation; whereby, "through grace," we "are saved by faith;" consisting of those two grand branches, justification and sanctification. By justification we are saved from the guilt of sin, and restored to the favour of God; by sanctification we are saved from the power and root of sin, and restored to the image of God.[5]

Prevenient grace

Wesley's order of salvation begins with his view of prevenient grace. This is grace that goes before salvation. Prevenient grace precedes convicting grace in Wesley's order of salvation. This grace is given to everyone, so that no man is in a totally natural state:

> There is no man, unless he has quenched the Spirit, that is wholly void of the grace of God. No man living is entirely destitute of what is vulgarly called *natural conscience*. But this is not natural: It is more properly termed *preventing grace*. Every man has a greater or less measure of this, which waiteth not for the call of man. Everyone has, sooner or later, good desires; although the generality of men stifle them before they can strike deep root, or produce any considerable fruit. Everyone has some measure of that light, some faint glimmering ray, which, sooner or later, more or less, enlightens every man that cometh into the world. And everyone, unless he be one of the small number whose conscience is seared as with a hot iron, feels more or less uneasy when he acts contrary to the light of his own conscience. So that no man sins because he has not grace, but because he does not use the grace which he hath.[6]

The above quotation indicates at least five things about Wesley's concept of prevenient grace. First, prevenient grace is given to all men, whether or not they ask for it. In this sense it is unavoidable. John 1:9 speaks of this light that enlightens everyone. Second, any good desire in any man proceeds from grace, even if only prevenient grace. Elsewhere, in a letter to his friend John Fletcher, Wesley spoke of the absolute necessity of the grace and Spirit of God to raise even a good thought or desire in a person's heart.[7] Third, though usually stifled, these desires do produce fruit when allowed to come to fruition. The fruit is not the product of man's working but is of God (man is cooperating with God's grace).[8] Prevenient grace is a divine enabling (that is usually squelched). Fourth, man is morally responsible for the prevenient grace that he is given. He sins when he does not use the grace he is given. Fifth, an individual sins against grace when he sins against his conscience. One's conscience functions by the grace of God.[9]

> **Wesley:**
> "No man sins because he has not grace, but because he does not use the grace which he hath."

In his sermon, "The Heavenly Treasure in Earthen Vessels," Wesley taught that prevenient grace, through the conscience, restores to man a measure of free will, so that he can now choose to respond to grace or to resist grace. Conscience provides for all men a degree of liberty.[10]

To Wesley, prevenient grace differs in *degree* from saving grace but not in its *nature*. It is always salvific.[11] It draws all men to salvation by preparing their hearts for convicting grace, or the gift of repentance.[12]

Wesley was careful to relate prevenient grace to the process of salvation. As stated in the introduction to this section, Wesley believed that prevenient grace (which included the first wish to please God, the first dawn of light concerning His will, and the first slight feeling of conviction for sin) implies a tendency toward life, some degree of salvation, and the beginning of a deliverance from a blind, unfeeling heart.[13]

Prevenient grace is something that all persons experience. If someone rejects this grace, he will incur upon himself the penalty for abusing the grace of God. If he responds, and by the power of the Holy

Spirit begins to seek God, God will grant him a deeper convicting grace, or repentance.

Prevenient grace is more than simply an attitude of favor on God's part
for the human race. It certainly is unmerited favor,[14] but it is also a divine

Wesley:
Grace is unmerited favor and an enabling power.

activity working in the human heart to enable someone to seek God (Titus 2:11).

Repentance

Repentance follows prevenient grace in Wesley's order of salvation. When someone responds to prevenient grace, God will give him more grace—repenting grace. Repentance as defined by Wesley is essentially self-knowledge. Repentance occurs when one sees how sinful and guilty he really is and how helpless he really is.[15] Convincing grace (the gift of repentance) convinces a person that he is an awful sinner, ripe for the judgment of God, and that there is nothing that he can do to remedy the situation. Repentance prepares someone for faith in that one must recognize his *sinfulness* before he will realize his need for salvation, and he must recognize his *helplessness*—that he cannot save himself—before he will cast himself on the mercy of the only one who can save him—Jesus Christ.

True repentance is conviction of sin. This implies contrition—a desire and a resolution to turn from sin.[16] True repentance will thus result in "works meet for repentance" (Acts 26:20). These works are actions that show that someone is serious about becoming a Christian. A person who is in the process of repenting will begin to make positive changes in his life—for example, he will begin to do good to his neighbor and will attempt to break with his sinful habits.[17] Wesley said that if one willingly neglects these works meet for repentance he cannot expect to be justified.[18]

These works meet for repentance, however, are only necessary as there is time and opportunity to do them. The process of repentance may last only for a short time for some people; these people may be able to exercise faith soon after they begin to repent. If so, there will be little or no opportunity to do works meet for repentance.[19] Those works, then, will become the fruit of a regenerate life.

Actually, though Wesley did expect those who were repenting to show proof that their repentance was real, he also encouraged penitents to trust Christ for salvation immediately. He told them that they should not wait until they felt contrite enough, or sincere enough, or good enough, or had done enough, before they took Christ at His word and believed for salvation.[20] They should immediately cast themselves on the mercy of Christ, exercising faith in Him for deliverance from sin.

> **Wesley:**
> True repentance implies a desire and a resolution to turn from sin.

Though Wesley strongly preached a message of repentance, he taught that neither repentance nor "works meet for repentance" carried with them any merit. They do not help one to earn his salvation. In his sermon "Justification by Faith," Wesley stated that repentance was nothing more or less than a deep sense of the lack of all good, and the presence of all evil.[21] Repentance actually involves a recognition that one has nothing or can do nothing to merit salvation.

Wesley also taught that, though repentance and "works meet for repentance" were necessary for salvation, they were not directly necessary; they were *in*directly necessary.[22] Faith is the only directly necessary condition for salvation because faith is what actually grasps onto the work of salvation, not repentance. Repentance is only necessary in that it must precede faith for faith to be real. Thus repentance and works meet for repentance are indirectly necessary.

There is another repentance that Wesley believed takes place in the life of someone who has already been saved.[23] This is a deeper repentance. Instead of one repenting of his sinful acts (a true Christian doesn't outwardly sin), he now "repents" of his sinful nature. He recognizes the awfulness of his depravity and his inward sins.[24] As he did when he first repented, he recognizes his helplessness. He realizes that he can do nothing to deliver himself from this sinfulness; that he must cast himself onto the Savior. This repentance will be referred to again when entire sanctification is discussed.

Saving Faith

Wesley defined Christian faith, the next step in the order of salvation, as not only an assent to the whole Gospel of Christ, but also a full reliance on the blood of Christ; a trusting in the merits of his life, death, and resurrection; a resting upon Him as our atonement and our life, as given for us and living in us. Faith is a sure confidence which a man has in God, that through the merits of Christ, his sins are forgiven and he is reconciled to the favor of God.[25] When someone trusts Christ for the forgiveness of sins, he is saved, or justified.

Faith presupposes repentance. One cannot believe without first repenting because one cannot cast himself totally on the mercies of Christ without first recognizing his sin and renouncing any good in himself. "True faith implies that the man comes to God as a lost, miserable, self-destroyed, self-condemned, undone, helpless sinner; he has renounced himself and any trust in his own works or righteousness of any kind."[26] The close relationship between faith and repentance is especially seen in this statement by Wesley: "Repentance disclaims the possibility of any other help; faith accepts all the help we stand in need of."[27]

Though Wesley stressed repentance, he believed, with the Reformers, in justification by faith alone. "Indeed, strictly speaking, the covenant of grace doth not require us to *do* anything at all, as absolutely and indispensably necessary, in order [for us to be justified]; but only to believe in Him."[28] Wesley said here and elsewhere that faith is the only necessary condition for justification. He explained this to mean that if a person has every spiritual quality but faith, he cannot be justified. But if a person who is considered to be lacking in every other spiritual quality exercises faith, he is justified.[29] Of course, this faith must be a true faith, and true faith presupposes an attitude of helplessness

> **Wesley:**
> True saving faith is faith
> that worketh by love.

concerning one's sinfulness and a willingness to turn from sin. But repentance does not take hold of justification—faith does.

Faith is a gift. Both the salvation and the faith of Ephesians 2:8 are considered by Wesley to be gifts.[30] God gives the faith and He helps the person to exercise that faith. This is necessary because one can do nothing without Christ. Since faith is a gift, it does not merit any of the favor of God; it does not earn one's salvation. The same has been said concerning repentance, which is also a work of God in the soul.

What are the fruits of true faith? True faith infallibly produces power over sin.[31] One cannot be exercising true saving faith and be rebelling against God through willful sin at the same time.[32] Faith will also inevitably produce the fruit of the Spirit and good works. True saving faith is faith that worketh by love (Galatians 5:6).[33] If faith does not bring forth love and all good works, it is not "the right living faith but a dead and devilish one."[34] Chapter six will more fully deal with this issue.

Wesley also taught that one must continue to believe in order to continue to be justified.[35] He believed it was absolutely necessary for there to be a response of the soul to God (the soul breathing back what it first received from God) in order for the divine life within (salvation) to continue.[36] Wesley said that faith is so vital to salvation, that if we were to cease believing, the next moment we could be devils:

> By faith we feel the power of Christ every moment resting upon us, whereby alone we are what we are; whereby we are enabled to continue in spiritual life, and without which, notwithstanding all our present holiness, we should be devils the next moment. But as long as we retain our faith in him, we draw waters out of the wells of salvation.[37]

Wesley is saying here that one only remains saved as the power of Christ rests upon the soul, and that the power of Christ can only rest upon the soul as one trusts Christ. If someone casts away his faith, the presence of Christ leaves. This results in spiritual death. The relationship between faith and salvation is such that one must continue to believe to continue to be saved.

Justification

When one truly believes, he is justified. Wesley defined justification as the act of God the Father by which He pardons, or forgives, penitent believers for the sake of His Son's human righteousness and propitiation. All of the *past* (not future) sins of those who believe are blotted out, and righteousness is imputed to their account. "By justification, we are saved from the guilt of sin, and restored to the favor of God."[38]

Justification is to be distinguished from sanctification. Justification is not being *made* actually righteous. Being made righteous is the act of sanctification. Justification is being *counted* as righteous.[39] However, Wesley believed that initial sanctification (the beginnings of sanctification) is *always* an immediate fruit of justification.[40] When God justifies someone, He does not deceive Himself into thinking that something is other than what it really is; considering someone righteous who is not.[41]

There were many in Wesley's day who thought that it was necessary to become holy before God would justify them. But, for at least two reasons, Wesley denied even the possibility of previous holiness being a condition for justification. First, Wesley believed that all truly good works follow justification. No works before justification can be good because they do not spring out of faith in Christ. Second, Christ justifies the *ungodly*, not the holy. If one were holy, it would be unnecessary for him to be justified. One must admit he is sinful before Christ will justify him. Furthermore, justification is based on what Christ did for man, not what man can do for Christ. Therefore, holiness and good works can neither precede justification nor be the conditions thereof.[42] One is justified by faith and faith alone.

Wesley made a distinction between initial justification (the justification we have been discussing up to this point) and final justification, which will occur at the final judgment.[43] Wesley believed that Paul and Jesus were referring to final justification when

> **Wesley:**
> Justification is by faith alone.

they said, "Not the hearers of the law, but the doers shall be justified" (Rom. 2:13), and "Every idle word you will give account for at the judgment" (Matt.12:36), and "By thy words you will be justified" (Matt.12:37). Wesley tried to explain these sayings of Jesus and Paul by suggesting that people will at the final day of judgment be justified in some way according to the grace-enabled works that were the fruit of their grace-enabled faith.

Though Wesley did believe that persons in some sense will be justified according to their works at the final judgment, he preached loudly and clearly that initial justification was purely conditioned on faith. At the end of Wesley's sermon "Justification by Faith," he pleads with hopeless, miserable sinners seeking justification, urging them to renounce their own righteousness[44] and look to Jesus:

> Thou ungodly one, who hearest or readest these words, thou vile, helpless, miserable sinner, I charge thee before God, the Judge of all, go straight unto him, with all thy ungodliness. Take heed thou destroy not thy own soul by pleading thy righteousness more or less. Go as altogether ungodly, guilty, lost, destroyed, deserving and dropping into hell; and thou shalt then find favour in his sight, and know that he justifieth the ungodly. As such thou shalt be brought unto the blood of sprinkling, as an undone, helpless, damned sinner. Thus look unto Jesus! There is the Lamb of God, who taketh away thy sins! Plead thou no works, no righteousness of thine own! No humility, contrition, sincerity! In no wise. That were, in very deed, to deny the Lord that bought thee. No: plead thou, singly, the blood of the covenant, the ransom paid for thy proud, stubborn, sinful soul. Who art thou, that now seest and feelest both thine inward and outward ungodliness? Thou art the man! I want thee for my Lord! I challenge *thee* for a child of God by faith! The Lord hath need of thee. Thou who feelest thou art just fit for hell, art just fit to advance his glory; the glory of his free grace, justifying the ungodly and him that worketh not. Oh come quickly! Believe in the Lord Jesus; and thou, even thou, art reconciled to God.[45]

Regeneration

When one exercises faith to be justified, he is also regenerated, or born again.[46] The term regeneration refers to the inward renewal that occurs in the heart of a believer when he is justified. Regeneration is an instantaneous work of God that brings spiritual life to a man and renews his fallen nature. It is man's (partial) restoration to the image of God.

> [Regeneration] is that great change which God works in the soul, when he brings it into life; when he raises it from the death of sin to the life of righteousness. It is the change wrought in the whole

soul by the almighty Spirit of God, when it is "created anew in Christ Jesus," when it is "renewed after the image of God, in righteousness and true holiness;" when the love of the world is changed into the love of God; pride into humility; passion into meekness; hatred, envy, malice, into a sincere, tender, disinterested love of all mankind. In a word, it is that change whereby the earthly, sensual, devilish mind is turned into the "mind which was Christ Jesus." This is the nature of the new birth.[47]

A distinction needs to be made between regeneration and justification. Justification is that which God does *for* a person; regeneration (the new birth) is that which God does *in* a person.[48] Regeneration is a real, actual change; justification is a relative change. In regeneration, the righteousness of Christ is imparted; in justification, the righteousness of Christ is imputed.

> **Wesley:**
> Justification and regeneration are simultaneous and inseparable.

These works of God are simultaneous and inseparable (one cannot happen without the other), though logically one is justified before he is regenerated.[49]

Wesley thought that the "born again" metaphor the Bible uses to describe regeneration is quite appropriate. Just as physical birth is instantaneous (basically), so the spiritual birth is instantaneous. Another similarity: before a baby is born physically, he cannot see or hear, though he has eyes and ears. Likewise, before someone is born spiritually, he cannot see or hear spiritually, though he has spiritual eyes and ears. Having no use of his spiritual senses, he has no true knowledge of God. But when one is born, whether physically or spiritually, his eyes and ears are opened. Also, when a baby is born physically, he begins to grow. When someone is born spiritually, he begins to grow (conforming to the image of Christ). In these ways, the spiritual birth is similar to the physical birth.[50]

Recognizing that regeneration is instantaneous (that one's spiritual eyes and ears are opened immediately) will help us to see that regeneration cannot be equated with sanctification.[51] Though they both refer to the inner renewal of man, they are not the same. Though someone is gradually *sanctified*, one does not become gradually *regenerated.* We could say, however, that one is *initially* sanctified in regeneration. The beginnings of sanctification occur in regeneration. Regeneration is "part of sanctification, not the whole. It is the gate to it, the entrance into it."[52] Sanctification will be discussed later in this chapter.

Wesley felt that regeneration was necessary because the new birth is a condition of holiness. No person could be holy without first being regenerated because holiness is more than bare external religion; holiness is the image of God stamped on the heart. This holiness can have no existence except through the new birth.[53]

Since regeneration is necessary for holiness, it is also necessary for eternal life, because the Bible says that without holiness no man shall see the Lord. If holiness is a condition for eternal life (seeing the Lord in Heaven) and regeneration is a condition for holiness, then it follows that regeneration is necessary for eternal life.[54]

What is a born again person like? Wesley describes him in a sermon entitled "The Marks of the New Birth." The first mark of the new birth is faith, a true living faith. An immediate and constant fruit of this faith is power over willful sin. Another fruit of faith is peace, a peace that keeps the hearts and minds of believers at all times and places. The second mark of the new birth is hope, a living hope.[55] Another name for this hope is the full assurance of faith (Hebrews 6:11; 10:22). This assurance that we are born of God includes the witness of our spirit and the witness of the Spirit of God. The third mark of those that are born of God is love of God. One fruit of this love of God is love for one's neighbor. Another fruit is obedience to Him that is loved, obedience to all of His commands.[56]

> **Wesley:**
> The constant fruit of a born again person's faith is power over willful sin.

Assurance

Assurance for Wesley was assurance that one is *now* in a state of salvation, not an assurance that one will *persevere* in that state.[57] Assurance is obtained through the witness of the Holy Spirit. This witness is confirmed by the witness of one's own spirit. The doctrine of the witness of the Spirit was very important to Wesley. He said that it was "one grand part" of the testimony which God had given the Methodists to bear to all mankind.[58] He thought that the doctrine of the witness of the Spirit was a great evangelical truth that had been recovered after many years of being almost totally lost and forgotten.[59] For Wesley, the witness of the Spirit was important because he felt that one would drift into a works-righteousness if he weren't personally assured by the Holy Spirit of his salvation. He said that any-

> **Wesley:**
> If someone denies the witness of the Spirit, he is, in effect, denying justification by faith.

one who denies the existence of the witness of the Spirit denies, in effect, justification by faith.

Wesley himself was assured of salvation by the witness of the Spirit on May 24, 1738. Here is his testimony:

> In the evening I went very unwillingly to a society in Aldersgate Street, where one was reading Luther's preface to the Epistle to the Romans. About a quarter before nine, while he was describing the change which God works in the heart through faith in Christ, I felt my heart strangely warmed. I felt I did trust in Christ, Christ alone for salvation; and an assurance was given me that He had taken away *my* sins, even *mine*, and saved *me* from the law of sin and death.[61]

This assurance of salvation was a result of experiencing the witness of the Spirit.

The witness of the Holy Spirit is defined by Wesley as "an inward impression of the soul, whereby the Spirit of God immediately and directly witnesses to my spirit, that I am a child of God; that Jesus Christ hath loved me, and given Himself for me; that all my sins are blotted out, and I, even I, am reconciled to God."[62] The witness of the Spirit is direct, immediate, and supernatural.

Wesley found the doctrine of the witness of the Spirit in Scripture. Two supporting verses are in Romans 8:15-16: "You received the Spirit of adoption by whom we cry out, 'Abba, Father.' The Spirit Himself bears witness with our spirit that we are children of God" (NKJ).

This witness, given when one trusts the word of God for salvation, is confirmed by the texts of Scripture which describe the marks of the children of God.[63] A true child of God, according to the Bible, knows he is a child of God because he keeps His commandments, loves the brethren, does righteousness, has the Spirit, and is led by the Spirit. These qualities enable him to have the testimony of a good conscience toward God. This testimony confirms the supernatural witness of the Holy Spirit. In other words, one will know that he is not deceived about the witness of the Spirit if he sees the fruit of the Spirit in his life. "The immediate fruits of the Spirit, ruling in the heart, are 'love, joy, peace, bowels of mercies, humbleness of mind, meekness, gentleness, long-suffering' [Galatians 5:22-23]. And the outward fruits are, the doing good to all men; the doing no evil to any; and the walking in the light—a zealous, uniform obedience to all the commandments of God."[64]

Wesley believed it was important not to confuse the fruits of the Spirit with the witness of the Spirit. If one thinks that the Spirit only witnesses to our spirit by the fruits of the Spirit, so that the witness and the fruits are one, he will slide back into justification by works.[65]

The witness of the Spirit is the privilege of every believer.[66] However, we must not say that someone is unsaved just because he doesn't have the witness. The witness of the Spirit, though very closely associated with faith, is not the same as faith, and therefore it is not absolutely essential to salvation, as faith is. Furthermore, the witness of the Spirit is at times not as strong as at other times.[67] When Christians go through trials or manifold temptations, the witness may grow weak and almost imperceptible.

> **Wesley:**
> Assurance is contingent on maintaining a faith relationship with God.

This does not mean one is not saved or is necessarily weak in faith.

It is possible that the witness of the Spirit be lost. It will inevitably be destroyed, not only by the commission of any outward sin, or the omission of known duty, but by yielding to any inward sin.[68] It seems that the witness of the Spirit and willful sin are mutually exclusive, as faith (with which the witness is closely associated) and willful sin are. Assurance, then, is contingent upon one's maintaining a faith relationship with God. As long as one continues to love God and keep His commandments, the testimony of his own spirit together with the testimony of God's Spirit confirm that he is the child of God.[69]

At the end of his sermon "The Witness of the Spirit," Wesley gives two warnings concerning assurance.[70] First, none should ever presume to rest in any supposed testimony of the Spirit which is separate from the fruit of it—the fruit of the Spirit. Second, none should rest in any supposed fruit of the Spirit without the witness. One who hasn't yet received the witness of the Spirit should be continually crying out to God until His Spirit cries in his heart, Abba, Father! (Romans 8:15)[71]

Sanctification

Sanctification is the process by which one is saved from the power and root of sin, and restored to the image of God.[72] Sanctification begins the instant someone is justified (this beginning is called initial sanctification or regeneration) and gradually increases until, in another instant, the heart is cleansed from all sin, and filled with pure love to God and man (this instantaneous work is called entire sanctification, or Christian perfection). Sanctification from that point gradually increases more and more until one "grows up into Him in all things" and attains the "measure of the fullness of Christ" (Ephesians 4:13-15).[73] Thus, sanctification is both gradual and instantaneous.

Entire sanctification (the cleansing from inbred sin) was the distinctive aspect of Wesley's doctrine of sanctification. Wesley believed that the doctrine of entire sanctification (or *Christian perfection* as he sometimes called it) was "the grand depositum which God has lodged with the people called Methodists; and for the sake of propagating this chiefly He appeared to have raised us up."[74]

> **Wesley:**
> Purification from inherited depravity can and should occur before death.

Entire sanctification as a work of God subsequent to justification is necessary because inbred sin remains in the heart of the believer even after he is regenerated.[75] Though most Christians in Wesley's day thought that sin must remain in one's heart until shortly before death, Wesley taught that purification from that sin could and should occur earlier.

Wesley believed that entire sanctification was not a new doctrine at all;[76] not only did many Christians throughout church history teach it, but also it was the doctrine of Jesus and the Apostles.[77] Wesley said that he found the doctrine of entire sanctification in the Old and New Testaments, when he read them with no other view or desire but to save his soul.[78] He saw entire sanctification promised in Ezekiel 36:25, 29: "Then will I sprinkle clean water upon you, and ye shall be clean: From all your filthiness, and from all your idols, will I cleanse you. I will also save you from all your uncleannesses." Paul plainly refers to this promise in 2 Cor. 7:1: "Having these promises, let us cleanse ourselves from all filthiness of flesh and spirit, perfecting holiness in the fear of God." Another promise fulfilled in the New Testament is Deut. 3:6: "The Lord thy God will circumcise thine heart, and the heart of thy seed, to love the Lord thy God with all thy heart and with all thy soul."[79] Wesley found certain prayers for sanctification in the New Testament that he thought would be mockery if there were no such thing as entire sanctification.

> **Wesley:**
> "If the love of God fill the heart, there can be no sin there."

These prayers included: "The very God of peace sanctify you wholly [entirely], and I pray God your whole spirit and soul and body be preserved blameless unto the coming of our Lord Jesus Christ" (I Thess. 5:23). Commands to the same effect are "Be ye perfect, even as your Father which is in heaven is perfect" (Matt 5:58), and "Thou shalt love the Lord thy God with all thy heart and with all thy soul, and with all thy mind" (Matt. 22:37).[80] According to Wesley, if one were to obey this last command (and one *can* obey, since God will not command anything His grace will not enable us to perform[81]), his heart would be entirely sanctified; for "if the love of God fill all the heart, there can be no sin there."[82]

Wesley described the "perfect" man (one who is entirely sanctified) in biblical terms. A perfect man is someone who is appropriating the promises of God for a holy heart and life.

> But what then…do you mean by one that is perfect…? We mean, one in whom is the mind which was in Christ, and who so walketh as

[Christ] walked; a man that hath clean hands and a pure heart; or that is cleansed from all filthiness of flesh and spirit; one in whom there is no occasion of stumbling, and who, accordingly, doth not commit sin. To declare this a little more particularly: We understand by that scriptural expression, a perfect man, one in whom God hath fulfilled his faithful word, From all your filthiness, and from all your idols, I will cleanse you. I will also save you from all your uncleannesses. We understand hereby, one whom God hath sanctified throughout, even in body, soul, and spirit; one who walketh in the light, as He is in the light, in whom is no darkness at all; the blood of Jesus Christ His Son having cleansed him from all sin.[83]

Wesley believed that God has fulfilled (from the time of the New Testament) His promises to cleanse hearts from all sin. The promises can be appropriated as a present reality, since God does not mock his children. And the commands can be obeyed since all commands are actually promises in disguise.[84] If God commands something, He expects us to appropriate the available grace that will enable us to obey the command. We should claim enablement to obey a command just as we claim promises since both commands and promises are the will of God.

Wesley used the word *perfect* to describe the entirely sanctified person because he considered it biblical: "Be ye perfect" (Matthew 5:48). "But as many as are perfect... (Phil. 3:15)." "Go on unto perfection" (Hebrews 6:1).[85] Perfection to Wesley did not mean maturity, but wholeness, or completeness.[86] Wesley clarifies what perfection is by showing what it is *not*:

Absolute and infallible perfection? I never contended for it. Sinless perfection? Neither do I contend for this, seeing the term is not scriptural. A perfection that perfectly fulfills the whole law, and so needs not the merits of Christ? I acknowledge none such—I do now, and always did protest against it.[87]

Most objections to Wesley's doctrine of perfection were due to misunderstandings of the term like those listed above. What Wesley meant by perfection was purity of intention,[88] not absolute conformity to the law of God or freedom from mistakes or infirmities.

Wesley said that perfect love was the essence of perfection and that "its properties, or inseparable fruits, are, rejoicing evermore, praying without ceasing, and in everything giving thanks" (I Thess. 5:16-18).[89]

He believed that perfection could be improved. "It is so far from lying in an indivisible point, from being incapable of increase, that one perfected in love may grow in grace far swifter than he did before."[90] However, not only can perfection be improved, but it also can be lost.[91]

To those who might think that an entirely sanctified person would no longer have need of Christ and the atonement, Wesley responded:

> **Wesley:**
> "One perfected in love may grow in grace far swifter than he did before."

The holiest of men still need Christ, as their Prophet, as "the light of the world." For He does not give them light, but from moment to moment; the instant He withdraws, all is darkness. They still need Christ as their King; for God does not give them a stock of holiness. But unless they receive a supply every moment, nothing but unholiness would remain. They still need Christ as their Priest, to make atonement for their holy things. Even perfect holiness is acceptable to God only through Jesus Christ... The best of men need Christ as their Priest, their Atonement, their Advocate with the Father; not only as the continuance of their every blessing depends on His death and intercession, but on account of their coming short of the law of love.[92]

Wesley acknowledged that, though he derived his doctrine of entire sanctification from the Scriptures, he depended in part on experience to confirm his interpretation of "holiness" passages. He said that if he and his preachers, after preaching this doctrine with such clarity and in so many places, never knew of any who experienced entire sanctification, he would reconsider his interpretation of those passages.[93] But his observation of the thousands in his Methodist societies that testified to the experience convinced him that reinterpretation of Scripture was unnecessary.[94]

Wesley taught that one can enter into this experience by repentance and faith.[95] Though one repents of his sins before he is saved, there is another repentance after salvation. This is a deeper repentance. It is not necessarily a knowledge of one's own sinful actions; it is a keen knowledge of one's own inherent depravity. It is a conviction (which implies contrition) of the tendency of one's heart to self-will, to atheism or idolatry, and above all, to unbelief. It is a conviction of the sin (not willful sin) that still remains in one's life, still cleaving to all his words and action. It is also a conviction of one's helplessness, of his utter inability to think any good thoughts, or say any right words, or do any good thing except by God's free grace.[96]

This repentance is always accompanied by works meet for repentance; that is, works of piety (attending the "means of grace"—religious services, Bible reading, prayer, communion, accountability meetings, etc.) and works of mercy. Wesley thought that if a person willingly neglects these fruits of repentance, he cannot reasonably expect ever to be entirely sanctified.[97]

Though repentance is a condition for entire sanctification, it is only an indirect condition. Faith is the direct condition. "Let a man have ever so much of this repentance, or ever so many good works, yet all this does not at all avail: he is not sanctified till he believes: but the moment he believes, with or without those fruits, yea, with more or less of this repentance, he is sanctified."[98]

Wesley described the faith necessary to become entirely sanctified as a divine evidence and conviction, first, that God has promised it in Scripture.

> Till we are thoroughly satisfied of this, there is no moving one step farther. And one would imagine there needed not one word more to satisfy a reasonable man of this than the ancient promise, "Then will I circumcise thy heart and the heart of thy seed, to love the Lord thy God with all thy heart, and with all thy soul, and with all thy mind" (Deut. 30:6). How clearly does this express the being perfected in love! How strongly imply the being saved from all sin! For as long as love takes up the whole heart, what room is there for sin therein?[99]

Faith is secondly a divine evidence and conviction that what God has promised He is able to perform. "Admitting, therefore, that 'with men it is impossible' to 'bring a clean thing out of an unclean,' to purify the heart from all sin, and to fill it with all holiness; yet this creates no difficulty in the case, seeing 'with God all things are possible.'"[100]

Faith is thirdly a divine evidence and conviction that God is able and willing to do it *now*. "And why not? Is not a moment to Him the same as a thousand years? He cannot want more time to accomplish whatever is his will. And he cannot want or stay for any more *wor-*

Order of Salvation	Stanley	Wesley
On Salvation	Salvation is the present possession of eternal life.	*Same as Stanley*
	Salvation includes deliverance from the guilt of sin and the consequence of sin—eternal death.	Salvation is not only deliverance from the guilt and consequence of sin, but also salvation from sin itself.
	Stanley limits his definition to a salvation which delivers persons from the guilt and consequence of sin. Stanley narrowly defines salvation as he does so that people will not think that one is saved or kept saved by not sinning.	Wesley emphasized that salvation is salvation from sin itself. One is saved from the consequences of sin only because he is saved from sin itself.
	Stanley will not accept a definition of salvation that implies that man has any responsibility for retaining his salvation.	Wesley recognized human responsibility, believing that salvation is conditioned upon a faith that works by love.
On Grace/ Prevenient Grace	Grace is unmerited favor. Grace is seen in those acts of kindness (particularly the work of Christ) that God has done for us in providing salvation. The offer of salvation is an act of grace.	*Same as Stanley*
	Stanley implies that someone can respond to the Gospel by his own strength.	Wesley had a concept of prevenient grace; that is, grace as the power of God working in the hearts of all men to enable them to begin to seek salvation.
On Repentance Before and After Salvation	Repentance for salvation is a change of mind about who Christ is and what He has done. It has nothing to do with repenting of one's sins. If it did, one might think that one's salvation is dependent upon behavior.	Repentance for salvation is recognizing one's sinfulness and helplessness. It implies contrition for sins committed and sincere resolutions to change. Works meet for repentance will follow.
	The repentance of those already saved is a repentance of sins that they commit. This repentance is very important to fellowship with Christ.	Repentance for believers is a recognition of one's inner depravity and one's helplessness to do anything about it. This deeper repentance deals with depravity rather than actual outward sins.

Continued...

Order of Salvation	Stanley	Wesley
...Continued		
On Faith	Faith is the only necessary condition for salvation (repentance is indirectly necessary). Faith is trust in Christ as the one who died for my sin and now forgives me (a personal trust). Trust involves both dependence and commitment.	*Same as Stanley*, though Wesley understood repentance and commitment to Christ differently. For Wesley, faith presupposes repentance *from sin*.
	Faith and sin can coexist.	Faith and sin are mutually exclusive—one cannot be exercising true saving faith in Christ and at the same time be rebelling against God through willful sin.
	Salvation and faith stand independently of one another; that is, one can have salvation without faith as long as he at one time expressed faith in Christ.	Salvation and faith must exist together in a dynamic relationship; only through a present faith can one be experiencing spiritual life (salvation).
	Stanley talks of faith purely in terms of man's response.	Faith itself is a gift of God. God gives sinners faith and helps them exercise that faith. It is the work of God as well as an act of man.
On the Fruit of Faith	Saving faith will not necessarily yield the fruit of the Spirit, especially since only an act of faith (without repentance from sin) is necessary to secure salvation eternally. Victory over sin and a fruitful Christian life are the results of being Spirit-filled, but not necessarily the results of exercising true saving faith in Christ.	The fruit of true saving faith is power over willful sin and a life producing the fruit of the Spirit and good works. True saving faith is faith that works by love. If faith isn't conquering sin and working by love, it is a dead faith.
On Justification	Justification is the act of God whereby He declares a sinner "not guilty" and imputes righteousness to his account. When one is justified, he is forgiven. Justification is by faith alone.	*Same as Stanley,* though Wesley said that only Christ's *passive* righteousness is imputed to us.

Order of Salvation	Stanley	Wesley
...Continued		
Justification	Past and future sins are forgiven when one is justified. Once a person is justified, he can never be subsequently found guilty.	Only *past* sins are forgiven when one is justified. One can forfeit his justified position through unbelief.
	Because Christ's righteousness is imputed to a person, one could still be actually unrighteous in real life and yet "be" righteous at the same time.	God always *implants* Christ's righteousness in the person to whom he *imputes* Christ's righteousness. There is no "legal fiction."
	One is born again when he is justified.	*Same as Stanley*
On Regeneration	Stanley says little about the nature of regeneration. He emphasizes justification, it seems, at the expense of regeneration.	Wesley emphasized that regeneration is the renewal of the image of God in a person (the beginning of sanctification) and that this renewal must occur if one is truly justified.
	A born again person has new life in Christ and is positionally free from sin (and therefore doesn't have to sin), but in reality he may be living in willful sin (grieving the indwelling Holy Spirit) and may go through a long process of repentance concerning those willful sins.	A born again person does not live in willful sin, but instead is always characterized by faith, hope, and love.
On Assurance	The privilege of every believer is the knowledge of his salvation.	*Same as Stanley*
	The Holy Spirit gives assurance of salvation.	*Same as Stanley*
On Assurance— Meaning and Basis	Assurance is the assurance that one is now saved and will persevere in his salvation (though not necessarily in holiness).	Assurance is a *present* assurance, a knowledge that one is *now* saved, but not that he will persevere.
	The basis of assurance is the acceptance of the doctrine of eternal security—the concept that if one is ever truly saved, he can never finally be lost. One does not need to have the fruit of the Spirit to have assurance of his final salvation.	The basis of assurance is on the witness of the Spirit, confirmed by the fruits of the Spirit (witness of *our* spirit, testimony of a good conscience toward God). One must not rest on one witness without the other.

Continued...

Order of Salvation	Stanley	Wesley
...Continued **On Sanctification**	Sanctification (being made holy) is an objective work done on the cross once for all.	Sanctification (being made holy) is a *subjective* work (done in the heart of a believer) which is *based* on the objective work of the atonement.
	The "flesh" of a Christian is nailed to the cross to die, but the flesh was nailed to the cross only in the objective sense. In real life, one will always struggle with sinfulness.	The death of the "flesh" (inherited depravity) can also happen in real life (in a subjective sense; that is, by the sanctifying grace at work in the heart of the Christian) before one physically dies.
	Since sanctification happened at the cross (an objective work), there is no way that one can lose sanctification.	Since sanctification happens in the heart of a believer, one can forfeit sanctification by rejecting the work of the Spirit.
	In real life, Christians can enter into the "wonderful, Spirit-filled life," a deeper experience with God subsequent to justification. This experience is entered into through a commitment to God and faith.	One enters into a deeper experience of sanctification (this deeper experience is called entire sanctification) when he "repents" of his inherited sinfulness, and trusts in Christ to cleanse him.
	The result of being Spirit-filled is a greater work of the Spirit in one's heart, which only continues as one continues in his commitment and faith.	The result of entire sanctification is freedom from inward depravity and the ability to love God with all one's heart. This work of God must be maintained by an obedient faith.
	It is in the Spirit-filled life (which may or may not begin at regeneration) that one gains victory over sin.	In regeneration one has already obtained victory over all willful acts of sin.
	It seems that Stanley describes the Spirit-filled life like Wesley describes regeneration, rather than entire sanctification.	

thiness or *fitness* in the person he is pleased to honor."[101]

Faith is last a divine evidence and conviction that He *does* it. "In that hour it is done: God says to the inmost soul, 'According to thy faith be it unto thee!'"[102]

To all this Wesley adds, "Expect it by *faith*, Expect it *as you are*, and Expect it *now!*"[103]

Evaluation

Please see comparison chart, pages 80-83, to better understand the following evaluation.

While we can appreciate Stanley's desire to help Christians become confident in their salvation, his redefinition of repentance and his assertion that one could be saved apart from a continued faith are of deep concern. He is teaching a distorted gospel message, essentially different from Wesleyan and classical Christian soteriology. Even John Calvin preached that initial repentance involved a repudiation of sin.[104] He also taught that the elect would at least exercise a thread of faith throughout their Christian experience.[105] Calvin never separated salvation from faith like Stanley has done. The important fact is that Stanley has compromised essential aspects of the gospel message.

It is evident that Stanley has tried to make basic soteriological definitions consistent with his doctrine of security. Repentance, faith, salvation, and sanctification have all been redefined to fit into his belief that a Christian can never be lost. Stanley ends up with unbiblical ideas. For example, to view sanctification as an imputed work is to completely misunderstand the work. Justification is the imputed righteousness; sanctification is *imparted* righteousness.

Stanley's interpretation of verses relating to faith deserves careful scrutiny. When he tries to refute the idea that one must continue to believe in order to continue to be saved, he shows a simplistic understanding of the Greek present tense. To determine how a present tense verb should be understood, there are three things to consider: the nature of the action, the context, and the grammar.[106] Stanley's illustration with the verb *live* actually works against him, for it *is* parallel to John's use of the verb *believe*. To "live in Atlanta" indicates a continuous, uninterrupted *residence* in Atlanta, but not a continuous presence. We can legitimately interpret the statement, "I live in Atlanta," to indicate that one's place of permanent (or continuous) residence is presently Atlanta. If one moved his place of residence to Chicago, but was staying the weekend in Atlanta, it would be untrue to say, "I live in Atlanta."

In the same way, John says those who are believing in Christ are saved. If, however, one has ceased believing in Christ, he does not meet the qualification for being saved. The consistent pattern of John's use of the present tense clearly underlines the necessity of a continuous, uninterrupted faith. If I am not right now trusting in Christ, I am in a state of unbelief. If I am in the state of unbelief I am under condemnation, according to John 3. Even Calvinist Leon Morris says that according to John 3, one will pass into a continuing state of condemnation if he refuses to enter a continuing state of belief.[107] Stanley does not properly interpret the scripture passages that teach us the necessity of *keeping* our faith in Christ.

We can appreciate Wesley's optimism of grace—his belief that God makes sanctifying grace available to us. God does not command us to do anything that we cannot now do by His enabling power. Paul's prayer for us to be entirely sanctified and kept until the day of Christ (I Thessalonians 5:23) is not a meaningless platitude. God intends to accomplish that work in us (I Thessalonians 5:24). Stanley has an incomplete view of grace, and he fails to understand how important it is for Christians to continually appropriate the grace available to them.

If Wesley's standard for regeneration is just a bit too high, Stanley's is far too low.[108] I John 3:9 (He who is born of God does not commit sin) has no meaning if it does not at least teach that a born-again Christian does not live in habitual willful sin.

Endnotes

1. *Works:* "Salvation by Faith," 5: 10-11.
2. *Works:* "Scripture Way of Salvation," 6: 44.
3. Ibid.
4. Ibid.

5. *Works:* "On Working Out Our Own Salvation," 6: 509.

6. Ibid., p. 512.

7. John Fletcher, *John Fletcher's Checks to Antinomianism.* Abridged by Rev. Peter Wiseman. (Kansas City: Beacon Hill Press, 1948), pp. 20. 21.

8. Wesley writes, "If we know and feel that the very first motion of good is from above, as well as the power which conducts it to the end; if it is God that not only infuses every good desire, but that accompanies and follows it, else it vanishes away; then it evidently follows, that 'he who glorieth' must 'glory in the Lord.'" *Works:* "On Working Out Our Own Salvation," 6:509.

9. *Works:* "On Conscience," 7:188-189.

10. *Works:* "The Heavenly Treasure in Earthen Vessels," 7:345.

11. By *salvific* I mean that the goal of prevenient grace is salvation, not that prevenient grace actually bestows the blessing of salvation.

12. "If we take [salvation] in its utmost extent, it will include all that is wrought in the soul by what is frequently termed, natural conscience, but more properly, preventing grace— all the drawings of the Father; the desires after God, which, if we yield to them, increase more and more;— all that light wherewith the Son of God 'enlighteneth everyone that cometh into the world;' showing every man, 'to do justly, to love mercy, and to walk humbly with his God;— all the convictions which his Spirit, from time to time, works in every child of man." *Works:* "Scripture Way of Salvation," 6:44.

13. Ibid.

14. As the following quote from Wesley shows, he did believe that grace was unmerited favor: "All the blessings which God hath bestowed upon man are of His mere grace, bounty, or favor; His free, undeserved favor; favor altogether undeserved; man having no claim to the least of His mercies. It was free grace that 'formed man of the dust of the ground, and breathed into him a living soul,' and stamped on that soul the image of God, and 'put all things under his feet.' The same free grace continues to us, at this day, life, and breath, and all things. For there is nothing we are, or have, or do, which can deserve the least thing at God's hands. 'All our works, Thou, O God, hast wrought in us.' These, therefore, are so many more instances of free mercy: and whatever righteousness may be found in man, this is also the gift of God." *Works:* "Salvation by Faith," 5:7.

15. *Works:* "The Way to the Kingdom," 5:81-82.

16. *Works:* "Principles of the Methodists Further Explained," 8:428.

17. Wesley described works meet for repentance as: "forgiving our brother, ceasing from evil, doing good, using the ordinances of God, and in general, obeying Him according to the measure of grace which we have received." *Works:* "Principles of Methodists Further Explained," 8:428.

18. *Works:* "Scripture Way of Salvation," 6:48.

19. Wesley taught that both repentance and faith were necessary for salvation, but they were necessary in a different sense and different degree. When Wesley said that works meet for repentance were necessary only as there were time and opportunity, he was showing how the necessity of these works differed from the necessity of faith in *degree.* *Works:* "The Scripture Way of Salvation," 6:48.

20. *Works:* "Righteousness of Faith," 5:74-76.

21. *Works:* "Justification by Faith," 5:61.

22. *Works:* "The Scripture Way of Salvation," 6:48. To say that repentance is indirectly necessary does not negate its importance. Repentance according to Wesley was definitely a

condition for salvation.

23. Wesley believed in two types of repentance. The first he named legal repentance, the second evangelical repentance. The first is a thorough conviction of sin—a recognition of one's sinfulness and helplessness, the second is a change of heart from all sin to all holiness. See *NT Notes:* "Matt 3:8."

24. This repentance would also include an awareness of one's guilt—because if it were not for the ever-atoning blood of Christ, one would be exposed every moment to fresh condemnation for the uncleanness attached to his unsanctified attitudes and actions (even though willful sins are not committed). *Works:* "Repentance of Believers," 5:163.

25. *Works:* "Salvation by Faith," 5:9, and *Works:* "Justification by Faith," 5:60-61.

26. *Works:* "Marks of the New Birth," 5:213-14. Elsewhere Wesley said, "We must be cut off from dependence upon ourselves, before we can truly depend upon Christ. We must cast away all confidence in our own righteousness, or we cannot have a true confidence in Him. Till we are delivered from trusting in anything that we do, we cannot thoroughly trust in what He has done and suffered. First we receive the sentence of death in ourselves; then, we trust in Him that liveth and died for us." *Works:* "Lord our Righteousness," 5:241.

27. *Works:* "Repentance of Believers," 5:168.

28. *Works:* "The Righteousness of Faith," 5:69.

29. *Works:* "Justification by Faith," 5:62.

30. That Wesley believed that the gift of salvation included the exercise of faith is shown by this statement: "Of yourselves cometh neither your faith nor your salvation: 'It is the gift of God;' the free, undeserved gift; the faith through which ye are saved, as well as the salvation, which he of his own good pleasure, his mere favour, annexes thereto. That ye believe, is one instance of his grace; that believing ye are saved, another. 'Not of works, lest any man should boast.' For all our works, all our righteousness, which were before our believing, merited nothing of God but condemnation. So far were they from deserving faith, which, therefore, whenever given, is not *of works.* Neither is salvation of the works we do when we believe; for *it is then God that worketh in us:* and, therefore, that he giveth us a reward for what he himself worketh, only commendeth the riches of his mercy, but leaveth us nothing whereof to glory." *Works:* "Salvation by Faith," 5:13.

31. "An immediate and constant fruit of this faith whereby we are born of God, a fruit which can in no wise be separated from it, no, not for an hour, is power over sin—power over outward sin of every kind; over every evil word and work." *Works:* "Marks of the New Birth," 5:214.

32. *Works:* "Minutes of Some Late Conversations, Mon. Jun 25, 1744," 8:276-77.

33. Wesley said that faith which does not produce both inward and outward holiness; the faith which does not stamp the whole image of God on the heart and purify us as He is pure; that faith that does not produce the whole of the religion described on the Sermon on the Mount is not the faith of the gospel, is not the Christian faith, and is not the faith which leads to glory. After preaching the preceding words, Wesley exclaimed: "Oh beware of this above all other snares of the devil, of resting on unholy, unsaving faith!" *Works:* "Sermon on the Mount XIII," 5:430-31.

34. *Works:* "The Almost Christian," 5:22.

35. "Continue to believe in Him that loved thee....Thus it is that we continue in a justified state." *Works:* "Repentance of Believers," 5:165.

36. *Works:* "Privilege of the Children of God," 5:232-33.

37. *Works:* "Repentance of Believers," 5:167.

38. *Works:* "On Working Out Our Own Salvation," 6:509.

39. *Works:* "Justification by Faith," 5:56-57.

40. Ibid., p. 56.

41. Ibid., p. 57.

42. Ibid., pp. 58-60.

43. Ibid., pp. 57-58.

44. As seen in this quotation, Wesley allowed no one seeking initial justification to plead his own righteousness. It must also be kept in mind that he taught that no one *ever* was to plead his own righteousness, even at the day of judgment. Justification is always based on the righteousness of *Christ.*

45. *Works:* "Justification by Faith," 5:64.

46. Wesley believed that the doctrines of justification and regeneration were two of the most fundamental of all doctrines. He said, "If any doctrines within the whole compass of Christianity may be properly termed 'fundamental,' they are doubtless these two." *Works:* "The New Birth," 6:65. Also worthy of note is the fact that the modern church owes to Wesley and Methodism the specific definition of regeneration that is now almost universally accepted by evangelical Protestants. Rev. N. Burwash, S.T.D., *Wesley's Doctrinal Standards* (Salem, OH: Schmul Pub., 1988), Introductory Notes by Editor, p. 173.

47. *Works:* "The New Birth," 6:71.

48. Ibid., p. 65.

49. Ibid., pp. 65-66.

50. Ibid., pp. 69-71.

51. Ibid., pp. 74-75.

52. Ibid., p. 74.

53. Ibid., pp. 71-72.

54. Ibid., pp. 69-71.

55. Wesley does not use the word "hope" in the sense of a "hope-so" salvation. Wesley speaks of hope not using its modern meaning but its biblical meaning—a full assurance of faith.

56. *Works:* "Marks of the New Birth," 5:213-20.

57. *Works:* "Letter to his Brother Samuel," 12:30.

58. *Works:* "Witness of the Spirit," 5:214.

59. Ibid.

60. Ibid., pp. 128-29.

61. *Works:* "May 24, 1738," 1:475-76.

62. *Works:* "Witness of the Spirit," 5:124-25.

63. Ibid., pp. 117-20.

64. Ibid., p. 124.

65. *The Letters of the Rev. John Wesley,* "To Samuel Furly," 5:8.

66. *Works:* "Witness of the Spirit," 5:134.

67. John Wesley, *A Plain Account of Christian Perfection,* (Kansas City: Beacon Hill Press, 1966), p. 86.

68. *Works:* "Witness of the Spirit," 5:134.

69. Ibid., p. 116.

70. Ibid., pp. 133-134.

71. Ibid., p. 124.

72. *Works:* "On Working Out Our Own Salvation," 6:509.

73. Ibid.

74. *The Letters of the Rev. John Wesley,* 8:238.

75. Wesley fully demonstrates this universally acknowledged truth in "Sin in Believers." *Works:* 5:144-56.

76. Wesley taught that if something was new it was not true. "But whatsoever doctrine is *new* must be *wrong*; for the *old* religion is the only *true* one; and no doctrine can be right, unless it is the very same 'which was from the beginning.'" *Works:* "Sin in Believers," 5:149.

77. *A Plain Account,* p. 117.

78. Ibid.

79. Ibid., p. 44.

80. Ibid., pp. 44-45.

81. Donald Thorsen, *The Wesleyan Quadrilateral,* (Grand Rapids: Zondervan, 1990), pp. 147-148. Thorsen quotes Outler who had outlined in his Introduction to the Bicentennial edition of the *Works* Wesley's principles of interpretation.

82. *Works:* "Minutes of Some Late Conversations, Wed. June 17, 1747," 8:296.

83. *Poetics:* "The Preface," 2:45-48.

84. See the note above concerning Wesley's principles of interpretation. Wesley considered all moral commands in the Bible as "covered promises."

85. From the KJV.

86. The Greek word translated 'perfect' in the New Testament is usually *teleios*, which means 'complete.'

87. *Works:* "A Plain Account of Christian Perfection," 11:369.

88. *A Plain Account,* p. 117.

89. Ibid., p. 114.

90. Ibid.

91. Ibid.

92. Ibid., pp. 82-83.

93. Ibid., p. 67.

94. To those that testified to the experience, Wesley gave seven pieces of advice in the tract, "Farther Thoughts on Christian Perfection." They are, in summary: First, watch and pray continually against pride. Second, beware of that daughter of pride, enthusiasm (fanaticism). Third, beware of Antinomianism; "making void the law" or any part of it, "through faith." Fourth, beware of sins of omission; lose no opportunity of doing good in any kind. Fifth, beware of desiring anything but God. Sixth, beware of schism, of making a rent in the Church of Christ. Seventh, be exemplary in all things. *A Plain Account,* pp. 95-105.

95. *Works:* "The Scripture Way of Salvation," 6:49-52.

96. Ibid., p. 51.

97. Ibid., pp. 48-51.

98. Ibid., p. 52.

99. Ibid.

100. Ibid.

101. Ibid.

102. Ibid., p. 53. With this came the witness of the Spirit. Wesley taught that just as one experiences the witness of the Spirit when he is justified, he also receives the witness of the Spirit when he is entirely sanctified. *A Plain Account*, p. 86.

103. *Works:* "The Scripture Way of Salvation," 6:53.

104. Concerning repentance, Calvin affirmed: "Wherefore, it seems to me, that repentance may be not inappropriately defined thus: A real conversion of our life unto God, proceeding from sincere and serious fear of God; and consisting in the mortification of our flesh and the old man, and the quickening of the Spirit." Calvin's *Institutes*: Book III, chapter 3, section 5.

105. Calvin stated: "Meanwhile, we must remember that however feeble and slender the faith of the elect may be, yet as the Spirit of God is to them a sure earnest and seal of their adoption, the impression once engraven can never be effaced from their hearts, whereas the light which glimmers in the reprobate is afterwards quenched. Nor can it be said that the Spirit therefore deceives, because he does not quicken the seed which lies in their hearts so as to make it ever remain incorruptible as in the elect." Calvin's *Institutes*: Book 3, chapter 2, section 12. "For the Spirit does not merely originate faith, but gradually increases it, until by its means he conducts us into the heavenly kingdom... Therefore, as we have already said, we again maintain, that faith remaining fixed in the believer's breast never can be eradicated from it. However it may seem shaken and bent in this direction or in that, its flame is never so completely quenched as not at least to lurk under the embers. In this way, it appears that the word, which is an incorruptible seed, produces fruit similar to itself. Its germ never withers away utterly and perishes." Calvin's *Institutes*: Book III, chapter 2, section 21.

106. Daniel B. Wallace, *Greek Grammar Beyond the Basics: An Exegetical Syntax of the New Testament* (Grand Rapids: Zondervan, 1996), 514-15, 556.

107. Leon Morris, *The Gospel according to John* in *The New International Commentary on the New Testament*, (Grand Rapids, MI: Wm. B. Eerdmans Publishing Co., 1995), p. 206. He says concerning John 3:18 (He who believes in Him is not condemned; but he who does not believe is condemned already), "The one of whom John writes has passed into a continuing state of condemnation on account of a refusal to enter a continuing state of belief."

108. Even classical theologians who believe that sin must remain in a believer his entire life will assert that regeneration brings dominion over it. I again quote John Calvin: "In regenerating his people God indeed accomplishes this much for them; he destroys the dominion of sin, by supplying the agency of the Spirit, which enables them to come off victorious from the contest. Sin, however, though it ceases to reign, ceases not to dwell in them." Calvin's *Institutes*, Book III, chapter 3, section 11.

6: WORKS

MUST GOOD WORKS FOLLOW FAITH?

A significant question debated throughout church history concerns the role of works in salvation. One's attitude toward works has always determined how (or if) he avoids the extremes of legalism and antinomianism. This chapter will show how Stanley and Wesley handle the role of works in salvation. The related subject of Christian liberty will also be discussed.

Stanley on Works

Stanley leaves no room for works in the obtaining or maintaining of salvation. He defines works in a very broad sense, making it refer to any human choice (other than an initial act of faith) that might be considered a condition for salvation. Though once thinking differently, Stanley now believes that if one could lose his salvation by choosing to do or not do something, then salvation is by faith and works, rather than by faith alone. Coming to this conclusion was a decisive factor in his conversion to a belief in eternal security.[1] Stanley came to the assumption that he would have to abandon his belief in salvation by faith alone if he continued to believe that one could lose

Charles Stanley:	John Wesley:
"If salvation is not forever, salvation cannot be through faith alone."	"If good works do not follow our faith, even all inward and outward holiness, it is plain that our faith is nothing worth; we are yet in our sin."

his salvation. It is his present position that works (which include not sinning) have no effect whatsoever on one's salvation or the maintenance of one's salvation. He insists that for works to play a role in the maintaining of one's salvation would leave room for boasting because it would mean that the daily burden of one's salvation rests on oneself.[2]

"Saying that God's grace enables us to maintain good works will not solve this dilemma. For who is responsible for daily appropriating that grace? We are back where we began. If salvation is not forever, salvation cannot be through faith alone."[3] To say that we are responsible for daily appropriating God's grace for salvation is to say that there are conditions for the maintenance of salvation. Of course, if there are any conditions that must be met, salvation is not free. "Having done nothing to earn [salvation], we can do nothing to lose it!"[4]

Stanley likens the person who believes that one can lose his salvation to the Pharisees, whose security was wrapped up in their ability to keep the law: "Like the Pharisees of old, some Christians believe their eternal security rests not on the finished work of Christ at Calvary but on the consistency of their good works."[5] They are like the Pharisee that Jesus said was trusting in himself for his security.

But isn't it true that people who believe they must maintain some kind of good works in order to *stay saved* are trusting in themselves for their eternal security? They can talk all they want about how they must depend on the power of God within them to walk the Christian walk. But the bottom line is that they *choose* to live a godly life; therefore, they are ultimately responsible for maintaining their salvation. If that is the case, we are saved by faith and kept by works. Thus, salvation is not a *gift*; it is merely an *opportunity*.[6]

> **Stanley:**
> If one has the responsibility of maintaining his salvation, salvation is partly by works.

For Stanley then, if salvation is conditioned on anything other than a single act of faith (which is a condition), then salvation is by faith plus works. If one has the responsibility of maintaining his salvation, no matter what the condition might be, salvation is partly by works. Salvation can only be a gift if there are no conditions that must be met in order to retain the gift. Meeting conditions for salvation is equivalent to working for salvation, which is equivalent to trying to earn salvation, which is absolutely contradictory to salvation by grace through faith alone.

Even maintaining faith would constitute works if continuing faith were a condition for continued salvation:

> If my faith maintains my salvation, I must ask myself, "What must I do to maintain my faith?" For to neglect the cultivation of my faith is to run the risk of weakening or losing my faith and thus my salvation. I have discovered that my faith is maintained and strengthened by activities such as the following: Prayer, Bible Study, Christian Fellowship, Church Attendance, and Evangelism. If these and similar activities are necessary to maintain my faith—and the maintenance of my faith is necessary for salvation—how can I avoid the conclusion that I am saved by my good works?[7]

If works even indirectly contribute to the maintenance of one's salvation through the cultivation of faith, one must conclude that he is saved by works and not by faith alone.

Stanley teaches that if there were any sins that would cause God to unadopt His children, then a person's salvation is contingent upon his *faith* and his *willingness* not to commit those particular sins.[8] Thus salvation would be by faith and works since one's willingness to repudiate sin is a form of works.

According to Stanley, those who feel they are responsible for maintaining their salvation (thus "working" for salvation) have a tendency to focus on their own behavior rather than on Christ. Those who constantly focus on their own behavior to examine their spiritual condition tend to fall into the trap of legalism. Legalism is almost always accompanied by self-deception (calling personal sins by some other name) and pride. Self-deception leads to greater and greater sin. The pride of these people results in a critical spirit. Many times those who are trying to maintain God's acceptance through good works (or by not doing certain things) end up giving up and living a life completely opposite of what they once stood for.[9] They would have been much better off having accepted their eternal security in Christ, and thus been enabled to focus more clearly on Him.

How does Stanley avoid a rank antinomianism that says, "Let us sin, that grace may abound"? He attempts to avoid it by teaching that sin still has eternal consequences. Believing that living a holy life has nothing to do with whether one is eternally saved or not does not prevent him from teaching that a man will reap what he sows. The God of all grace who loves His children unconditionally is also a God of justice. He will give to every man his just due. Though sin will not separate a Christian from God, it can prevent him from gaining the rewards that he could have gotten had he remained faithful. The unfaithful Christian will hold a lesser position in heaven than those who will have remained true.

> **Stanley:**
> Outer darkness is not hell; it is a sphere of lesser privilege in heaven for the unfaithful.

When Jesus spoke of the outer darkness into which the unfaithful servant was cast, He was not referring to hell; He was referring to a lesser sphere of influence and privilege. "To be in the 'outer darkness' is *to be in the kingdom of God but outside the circle of men and women whose faithfulness on this earth earned them a special rank or position of authority.*"[10] Stanley explains the "weeping and gnashing of teeth" associated with this "outer darkness": "Just as those who are found faithful will rejoice, so those who suffer loss will weep. As some are celebrated for their faithfulness, others will gnash their teeth in frustration over their own shortsightedness and greed."[11] At some point God will comfort these persons who have suffered loss (Rev. 21:4), but they will never have the rewards of the faithful. The rewards given out will be permanent.[12]

Again, eternity will not be the same for every Christian. I Corinthians 3:11-15 describes the work of two men who built upon the same foundation (Christ) but who built upon that foundation using very different materials. The first man used gold, silver, and precious stones; the other wood, hay, and straw. The gold, silver, and precious stones endured the flame of testing, but the wood, hay, and straw burnt up. Whereas the first man had a great reward in heaven, the second man suffered loss and went into heaven smelling of smoke.[13] The first man represents those who have made real contributions to God's kingdom during their earthly lives and thus are rewarded for their faithfulness. The second man represents those believers who have lived for themselves rather than for Christ. In the end, nothing they have lived for has counted. Though they are eternally saved (I Cor. 3:15) they will not have the rewards that the faithful believers will have.[14]

> Within [God's] plan of salvation there are special rewards for those who respond to Him in like kind. Great is their reward in heaven. Eternity will not be the same for every believer. We will all stand and give an account of our lives. We will be judged according to our deeds, whether good or bad. Our rank in His future kingdom is being decided each and every day of our lives.
>
> For those who have as their ambition to be pleasing to the Lord, this comes as great news. For those who are seeking to have their cake and eat it too, this is rather disheartening. And so it should be. God is not One to be mocked. There are no loopholes in His economy. Even within the context of His grace, we will still reap what we sow. But that sword cuts both ways. For those who sow seeds of faithfulness and obedience, their crop will yield enduring fruit. For those who sow seeds of disobedience and selfishness, their crop will fail to endure the fiery judgment. They will have nothing to show for their lives. They will be poor in the kingdom of heaven.[15]

Christian Liberty

According to Stanley, the Christian has been freed from the law (all the Mosaic Law) as a result of the offer of grace. Ever since Jesus came and fulfilled the law, a person no longer is justified on the basis of keeping the law, but solely by the grace of God. We are now "under grace," not "under the law." To be "under the law" means to keep the law in order to become or stay saved. A person in this dispensation of grace nullifies the grace of God when he tries to keep the law as a means

Stanley:
"Law and grace do not mix."

of attaining or maintaining salvation. This person is trying to join works and grace. But, "law and grace do not mix."[16] If one would try to integrate portions of the law (any part of the Mosaic Law) into the gospel, he would nullify the need for Christ's death.[17] A person with true Christian liberty realizes that he need not keep any part of the law to be justified or to stay justified. He moves again under the bondage of the law when he thinks that keeping part of the law contributes to his salvation in any way. A real Christian who makes this mistake loses his freedom, but he doesn't lose his salvation.

Wesley on Works

Wesley clearly aligned himself with the Protestant teaching that a man is justified by faith and not by works. According to Wesley, all our works and all our righteousness before we believe merit nothing but condemnation. Even after we believe, our works merit nothing because it is God that worketh in us, and, "therefore, that he giveth us a reward for what he himself worketh, only commendeth the riches of his mercy, but leaveth us nothing whereof to glory."[18]

It is not possible that one could be partially justified by grace through faith and partially by works, because the concept of being justified by grace and the concept of being justified by works are totally incompatible.

> There is something so absolutely inconsistent, between the being justified by grace, and the being justified by works, that if you suppose either, you of necessity exclude the other. For what is given to works is the payment of a debt; whereas grace implies an unmerited favor. So that the same benefit cannot in the very nature of things, be derived from both.[19]

One must choose to believe either that one is justified by works or that one is justified by grace. Wesley chose to accept the biblical teaching of salvation by grace through faith alone.

From beginning to end, one is saved by trusting in the merits of Christ, not his own merits. One cannot trust in the merits of Christ until he has totally renounced his own.[20] He forfeits his relationship with God if he ceases to trust in the merits of Christ and again trusts in his own righteousness.

Though Wesley boldly preached justification by faith, he also tried to be careful to strike a balance between the extremes of antinomianism and pharisaism:

The truth lies between both. We are doubtless, justified by faith. This is the cornerstone of the whole Christian building. We are justified without the works of the law, as a previous condition of justification: but they are an immediate fruit of that faith, whereby we are justified. So that if good works do not follow our faith, even all inward and outward holiness, it is plain that our faith is nothing worth; we are yet in our sin.[21]

Works, therefore, are not a condition of justification but an inevitable, immediate, and necessary fruit of justification. Verses of Scripture that say that we must live a holy life in order to enter heaven and verses that say that we are saved by grace through faith are not contradictory when one considers the true relationship between faith and works. Wesley says,

> **Wesley:**
> For works and faith so often to be set opposed to each other is a device of Satan.

Some have supposed that when I began to declare "By grace ye are saved through faith," I retracted what I had before maintained: "Without holiness no man shall see the Lord." But it is an entire mistake. These scriptures well consist with each other; the meaning of the former being plainly this—By faith we are saved from sin, and made holy.[22]

Wesley felt like it was a "very device of Satan" that works and faith were often set to oppose one another. He thought that many who had a real zeal for God fell into this snare of Satan (at least for a time) at either extreme:

> Some have magnified faith to the utter exclusion of good works, not only from being the cause of our justification, (for we know that a man is "justified freely by the redemption which is in Jesus,") but from being the necessary fruit of it, yea, from having any place in the religion of Jesus Christ. Others, eager to avoid this dangerous mistake, have run as much too far the contrary way; and either maintained that good works were the cause, at least the previous condition, of justification, or spoken of them as if they were all in all, the whole religion of Jesus Christ.[23]

The balanced position is that one is justified by a faith that works. Works are the necessary fruit of justification by faith.

Though Wesley believed in salvation by faith alone, he also believed that works do have a role in the maintenance of one's salvation. Though no merit whatsoever is acquired by a Christian by anything he does or does not do, a Christian's choices will cause him to forfeit or to maintain saving faith. Wesley's position is stated in the Methodist Society's Minutes of 1744, where the following questions and answers were presented:

> **Q**: Are works necessary to the continuance of faith?
> **A**: Without doubt; for a man may forfeit the free gift of God, either by sins of omission or commission.
> **Q**: Can faith be lost but for want of works?
> **A**: It cannot be but through disobedience.[24]

Works, then, are seen as necessary for the continuance of faith (and thus salvation) when works are understood to mean what one does to live in obedience to the known will of God. It is not *the lack* of works *itself* that will cause one to forfeit his faith, but willful disobedience to the known will of God. Faith cannot long abide in a heart which sins presumptuously or which willfully persists in a train of omissions (without repentance).[25]

Wesley thought that Phil. 2:12,13 helped to explain the role of works in salvation: "Work out your own salvation... For it is God that worketh in you both to will and to do of his good pleasure." The connection between our working and God's working is that it is God that worketh in us both to will and to do; therefore, we must work out our own salvation. God's working in us both to will and to do means that "He breathes into us every good desire, and brings every good desire to good effect."[26] Knowing that it is God that is producing these desires and effects should hide pride from us. If we realize that we have nothing that we have not received, how can we glory as if we had not received it? "If we know and feel that the very first motion of good is from above, as well as the power which conducts it to the end; if it is God that not only infuses every good desire, but that accompanies and follows it, else it vanishes away; then it evidently follows, that 'he who glorieth' must 'glory in the Lord.'"[27]

There is no contradiction between God working in us and our working. Instead, there is a close connection. Since God works, we *can* work. If God didn't work in us, it would be impossible for us to work out our own salvation. Just as it was impossible for Lazarus to come forth, until Jesus had given him life, so it is "equally impossible for us to *come* out of our sins or to make the least motion toward it, till He who hath all power in heaven and earth calls our dead souls into life."[28] But this is no excuse for any to continue in their sins, because God has given grace to everyone. If persons respond to the grace God has already given them, He will give them more grace. "No man sins because he has not grace, but because he does not use the grace which he hath."[29] Since God is working in us, we can work out our own salvation. This means that it is possible for us to fulfill all righteousness, loving God and walking in love.

Not only is it *possible* for us to work out our salvation, but it is also *necessary*. Since God works in us, we *must* work out our salvation. We must be workers together with Him or He will cease working. "Unto him that hath shall be given but he that hath not from him shall be taken away that which he hath" (Mark 4:25). In other words, if one does not improve the grace already given, the grace he has already been given will be taken away. "Even St. Augustine, who is generally supposed to favor the contrary doctrine, makes that just remark…'He that made us without ourselves, will not save us without ourselves.'"[30]

Christian Liberty

Wesley encouraged believers to enjoy their Christian liberty. "Thou are not only made free from Jewish ceremonies, from the guilt of sin, and the fear of hell; (these are so far from being the whole, that they are the least and lowest part of Christian liberty;) but what is infinitely more, from the power of sin, from serving the devil, from offending God."[31] For Wesley, Christian liberty is much more than freedom from the Jewish ceremonial law; Christian liberty is primarily freedom from the bondage of sin.[32] It is not freedom from the moral law of God; it is freedom to *keep* the moral law of God, by having power to obey His commands, and thus please God.

It becomes evident that Christian liberty is not freedom from the moral law when one considers what the moral law is. The law of God (the moral law) is "a copy of the eternal mind, a transcript of the divine nature, yea, it is the fairest offspring of the everlasting Father, the brightest efflux of his essential wisdom, the visible beauty of the Most High."[33] It is that law that God promised to write into the hearts of those whose iniquities He had forgiven. Three of the properties of this law are: It is holy, just, and good (Romans 7:12). The uses of this moral law are: 1) It convinces the world of sin. It slays the sinner—it destroys the life and strength wherein he trusts and convinces him that he is dead in sin. 2) As schoolmaster, it brings the sinner unto life—unto Christ, that he may live. 3) It keeps alive those that come to Christ. "It is the grand means whereby the blessed Spirit prepares the believer for larger communications of the life of God... It is continually exciting all believers, the more they see of its height, and depth, and length, and breadth, to exhort one another so much the more."[34]

> **Wesley:**
> Christian liberty is not freedom from the moral law of God; it is freedom to keep the moral law of God.

Every believer is done with the law; if what is meant is the Jewish ceremonial law or the Mosaic dispensation as a whole. Christ has taken these out of the way. Even the moral law is unnecessary as a means of procuring a person's justification since we are justified freely by His grace.[35] But there is a sense in which the Christian is not done with the moral law[36]: the law convicts the Christian of sin that remains in his heart and life and thereby keeps him close to Christ, so that His blood may cleanse him every moment. The law also acts as a promise of what Christ's grace will do for the Christian (Romans 8:4 —"That the righteousness of the law might be fulfilled in us"):

> I cannot spare the law one moment, no more that I can spare Christ: seeing I now want it as much, to keep me to Christ, as I ever wanted it to bring me to him. Otherwise, this "evil heart of unbelief" would immediately "depart from the living God." Indeed each is continually sending me to the other, the law to Christ, and Christ to the law. On the one hand, the height and depth of the law constrain me to fly to the love of God in Christ; on the other, the love of God in Christ endears the law to me "above gold or precious stones;" seeing I know every part of it is a gracious promise, which

my Lord will fulfill in its season.[37]

Wesley saw no contradiction between the moral law and the gospel; they are not opposed to each other in the least. In fact, the very same words in Scripture can be considered as either part of the gospel or part of the law:

> If they are considered as commandments, they are parts of the law; if as promises, of the gospel. Thus, "Thou shalt love the Lord thy God with all thy heart," when considered as a commandment, is a branch of the law; when regarded as a promise, is an essential part of the gospel; the gospel being no other than the commands of the law, proposed by way of promise.[38]

This view of the law and gospel results from considering the moral commands in scripture as actually promises under cover (in disguise) that Christ expects to be fulfilled in the Christian's life. Laws are "promises" because God makes available the grace to enable anyone to keep his commands. As you would expect from someone with such a high view of the law, Wesley was very concerned when he saw Christians begin to "make void the law by faith" by teaching that Christians are free from the moral law.

> **Wesley:**
> "The gospel is none other than the commands of the law, proposed by way of promise."

A Christian violates true Christian liberty when he makes "void the law by faith." One way to pervert Christian liberty by making void the law by faith is to not preach the law at all.[39] Another way is to teach that faith supersedes the necessity of holiness, saying that holiness is less necessary now than it was before Christ came.[40]

Paul the Apostle warned Christians not to make void the law through faith when he said, "Shall we sin because we are not under the law, but under grace? God forbid" (Romans 6:15). Wesley thought that we should understand thoroughly what Paul meant when he spoke of Christians not being "under the law" but "under grace." Being "under the law" could mean in the above verse: first, the obligation to observe the ceremonial law; second, the obligation to conform to the whole Mosaic institution; third, the obligation to keep the whole moral law, as the condition of one's acceptance with God; and fourth, being under the wrath and condemnation of God, having a sense of guilt and fear.[41]

A believer is not "under the law" in any of the four senses described above. Instead, he is "under grace":

> As he is no longer under the ceremonial law, nor under the Mosaic institution; as he is not obliged to keep even the moral law, as the condition of his acceptance; so he is delivered from the wrath and the curse of God, from all sense of guilt and condemnation, and from all that horror and fear of death and hell, whereby he was all his life before subject to bondage. And he now performs (which while "under the law" he could not do) a willing and universal obedience. He obeys not from the motive of slavish fear, but on a nobler principle; namely, the grace of God ruling in his heart, and causing all his works to be wrought in love.[42]

Now that one being "under grace" serves God out of love rather than fear, he cannot assume that he is less obligated to be holy than before. "Shall this evangelical principle of action be less powerful than the legal? Shall we be less obedient to God from filial love, than we were from servile fear?"[43] Many Christians, though not making void the law through faith in theory (i.e. by what they say they believe), do so in their practice when they begin to be more careless, or less obedient, in their living than when they were "under the law," or "under conviction."

> **Wesley:**
> "I defy all liberty but liberty to love and serve God, and fear no bondage but bondage to sin."

Many people, when they were under the condemnation of the law, were much more conscientious in how they indulged the flesh, in how they dressed, in how they conversed with their neighbor, in how they spent their money, and in how they attended the means of grace. But now that they are "under grace," they have become a little careless. This is a dangerous mistake. They were not *too* conscientious *before*; instead, they are *not enough so now* and are in danger of "turning the grace of God into lasciviousness." They must repent and live by a different principle. "Is love a less powerful motive than fear? If not, let it be an invariable rule, 'I will do nothing now I am under grace, which I durst not have done when under the law.'"[44]

In his sermon "Witness of the Spirit," Wesley describes the self-deceived person, who thinks he is saved when he is not. This person, having a false view of Christian liberty, believes that he has the liberty to disobey the commands of God. He therefore is less zealous of good works than he was when he was "under the law," or under conviction. He believes that since he is at liberty, he is no longer obligated to observe the law. Consequently, he no longer exercises himself unto godliness. He has found an easier way to heaven.[45]

The antinomians in Wesley's day taught that one branch of Christian liberty was liberty from obeying the commandments of God. To the antinomians, someone was in bondage if he did a thing because it was commanded or did not do something because it was forbidden.[46] This was a perverted view of Christian liberty according to Wesley. He said that he feared no bondage except bondage to sin. And he rejected all concepts of liberty but liberty to love and obey God.[47]

Wesley took to task some of the Moravians of his day who said that they believed that Christian salvation implied liberty to conform to the world, by putting on of gold and costly apparel, contrary to I Timothy 2:8-10 and I Peter 3:3-5.[48] Wesley believed that Christian liberty was not liberty to disregard commands of Scripture that had not been taken away by Christ.

Evaluation

Please see comparison chart, pages 104-105, to better understand the following evaluation.

Though Wesley correctly distinguished between the meeting of the conditions for salvation and the seeking to earn salvation through works, Stanley equates these two concepts. Stanley's view of works supports unconditional eternal security because he considers as works any choice one makes to do what God requires. Once one believes, there is nothing he could choose to do or not do that could separate him from God, since one is not saved by works. But Stanley is not consistent with the way he defines works when he discusses the initial act of faith. The initial act of faith, Stanley's only condition for

Works	Stanley	Wesley
On the Place of Works in Salvation	There is no merit for salvation earned through works. All good works follow justification and contribute nothing to the gift of salvation.	*Same as Stanley*
On the Necessity of Works that Follow Justification	Works should follow justification. The consequence of not "working out one's salvation" (or being obedient) is a subordinate role in heaven. For Stanley, whether someone who has accepted Christ "works" or not has no bearing on his eternal destiny.	Works *must* follow justification. For Wesley, the consequence of not "working out one's salvation" (or being obedient) is spiritual death; For Wesley, one may forfeit his salvation by failing to "work," or by refusing to live a life obedient to Christ. One can destroy his faith (and thus forfeit his salvation) by willfully sinning and refusing to repent.
On the Attempt to Avoid Antinomianism	Living a holy life is necessary to secure a place of high honor in heaven, though not necessary to enter heaven. One will be rewarded in heaven according to his works.	Though one is saved by grace through faith alone, true faith will inevitably produce the fruit of a holy life. It is through faith that one is made actually holy and thus made fit for heaven, where he will be rewarded for his deeds.
On the Attempt to Avoid Legalism	Since faith for salvation is a single act of trust, works cannot contribute to salvation even indirectly. Even faith cannot be an ongoing condition for salvation. If it were, works would somehow be inserted into the salvation process indirectly, by works that cultivated faith.	Salvation is by grace through faith alone. Works do not and cannot contribute to one's salvation; salvation is purely by grace through faith. Any works that a Christian is able to perform are not his own anyway; they are the result of God's working in the Christian's heart and life. Since God is the One actually doing the work, no works earn merit for man; all the honor for any work the Christian performs goes to God.
On the Meaning of Christian Liberty	Freedom *from* the law is the primary meaning of Christian liberty. Christians must not be in bondage to the law (rules). Stanley thinks that Christians are legalistic if they think they must meet any conditions to maintain their salvation.	Christian liberty is primarily liberty of desire and ability to *keep* the law (the moral law). Christians must not be in bondage to sin. Salvation is continuously conditional. One is an antinomian if he teaches that living a holy life (from a heart regenerated by grace through faith) is not necessary to get to heaven.

Continued...

Works	Stanley	Wesley

...Continued

Works	Stanley	Wesley
On the Law and the Gospel	For Stanley, the law and gospel are at opposite poles. They "cannot mix."	The moral law and the gospel are at the same "pole." Many verses of Scripture could be said to be either part of the law or part of the gospel, depending on whether they are considered commands or promises. Actually, commands (law) are promises (gospel) under cover.
	The law is a schoolmaster to bring someone to Christ. Only one who knows he is a sinner can accept Christ's gift of salvation.	The law is that which not only *brings* one *to* Christ, but that which also *keeps* him *with* Christ.

salvation, is a "work" by his definition, because faith is something that one chooses to do. He is inconsistent because he equates meeting conditions for salvation with trying to earn salvation, yet he allows one exception—the initial choice to believe.

Romans 4:3-5 makes it clear that faith is not a work ("But to him that worketh not, but believeth on him that justifieth the ungodly, his faith is counted for righteousness"). For Wesley to insist that faith must continue in the life of a Christian is obviously not inconsistent with justification by faith alone.

Stanley's unique interpretation of the passage that teaches that the unfaithful will be cast into 'outer darkness' is a gross abuse of the text. The passage clearly implies lostness. Consider: God is light; there is no darkness in him. How can there be outer darkness in heaven? Stanley has deliberately twisted Scripture's plain meaning to make it fit his theological preconception.

Stanley thinks that because he teaches that unfaithful Christians will receive fewer rewards, he avoids the error of antinomianism. However, his position is essentially antinomian. He teaches that the only condition for salvation is a single act of faith. Repentance from sin is not required, even at the moment of conversion. People who "accept Christ" can expect to be saved even if they never obey any commands from the moral law. This is pure antinomianism. Stanley's teaching, regardless of what is said about rewards, allows many to be deceived about their relationship with Christ.

John Wesley has a more accurate view of Christian liberty, seeing it as both freedom from the law as a means of salvation and freedom to obey God's moral law through enabling grace. Stanley sees Christian liberty as freedom from being required to keep even God's moral law. Stanley's position is at odds with Romans 6:15 ("Shall we sin because we are not under law but under grace? God forbid"). What is this sin, but a willful violation of God's moral law? Stanley's teaching is likely to breed an unhealthy attitude toward the commands in Scripture, and thus encourage carelessness in applying Christian ethics to everyday living.

The bottom line: Stanley misunderstands the biblical meaning of "works" and the true relationship between the law and the gospel. Thus, he has been led into the classic error of antinomianism.

Endnotes

1. *Eternal Security,* p. 4.
2. Ibid., p. 11.
3. Ibid.
4. Ibid., p. 90.
5. Ibid., p. 45.
6. Ibid., p. 54, footnote 1.
7. Ibid., p. 87.
8. Ibid., p. 43.
9. Ibid., p. 13.
10. Ibid., p. 126.
11. Ibid., p. 127.
12. Ibid., p. 128.
13. Tape 6, "What Do We Have To Lose," *Eternal Security.*
14. *Eternal Security,* pp. 120-21.
15. Ibid., pp. 193-94.
16. Ibid., p. 139.
17. Ibid., p. 140.
18. *Works:* "Salvation by Faith," 5:13.
19. *Notes on the New Testament:* "Romans 11:6."
20. *Works:* "Salvation by Faith," 5:14.
21. *Works:* "Law Established by Faith," 5:453-54. Further advice by Wesley on avoiding the extremes of pharisaism and antinomianism was recorded by Fletcher in his Checks [John Fletcher, *Checks to Antinomianism,* abridged by Rev. Peter Wiseman, (Kansas City: Beacon Hill Press, 1948), p. 22]: "Avoid all extremes. While on the one hand you keep

clear of the Pharisaic delusion that slights Christ, and makes the pretended merit of an imperfect obedience the procuring cause of eternal life; see that on the other hand you do not lean to the antinomian error, which, under pretense of exalting Christ, speaks contemptuously of obedience, and 'makes void the law' through a faith that does not 'work by love.' As there is but a step between high Arminianism and self-righteousness, so there is but one between high Calvinism and Antinomianism. I charge you to shun both, especially the latter."

22. *Works:* "On the Wedding Garment," 7:317.

23. *Works:* "Upon Our Lord's Sermon on the Mount," Discourse VII., 5:344-45.

24. *Works:* "Minutes of Some Late Conversations, Mon., June 25, 1744," 8:276-77.

25. *Works:* "The Wilderness State," 6:80-81.

26. *Works:* "Working Out Our Own Salvation," 6:508.

27. Ibid., p. 509.

28. Ibid., p. 513.

29. Ibid., p. 512.

30. Ibid., p. 513.

31. *Works:* "The Original, Nature, Property, and Use of the Law," 5:446.

32. Wesley says in one of his letters, "I defy all liberty but liberty to love and serve God, and fear no bondage but bondage to sin." John Wesley, London, Nov. 30, 1770, to Joseph Benson in *The Letters of the Rev. John Wesley,* 5:211-212.

33. *Works:* "The Original, Nature, Property, and Use of the Law," 5:439.

34. Ibid., p. 443.

35. Ibid., p. 444.

36. Wesley is certainly with Calvin at this point. Concerning Christian liberty, John Calvin said, "Still it cannot be rightly inferred from this that believers have no need of the law. It ceases not to teach, exhort, and urge them to good, although it is not recognized by their consciences before the judgment-seat of God. The two things are very different, and should be well and carefully distinguished. The whole lives of Christians ought to be a kind of aspiration after piety, seeing they are called unto holiness (Eph. 1: 4; 1 Thess. 4: 5). The office of the law is to excite them to the study of purity and holiness, by reminding them of their duty." Calvin's *Institutes*, Book III, chapter 19, section 2.

37. Ibid., p. 445.

38. *Works:* "Upon Our Lord's Sermon on the Mount Discourse Five," 5:313.

39. *Works:* "Law Established by Faith," 5:449.

40. Ibid., p. 452. To those who would respond to these statements with: "But are we not justified by faith, without the works of the law?" Wesley says, "Undoubtedly we are, without the works either of the ceremonial or the moral law. And would to God all men were convinced of this! It would prevent innumerable evils; Antinomianism in particular: for, generally speaking, they are the Pharisees who make the Antinomians. Running into an extreme so palpably contrary to Scripture, they occasion others to run into the opposite one. These, seeking to be justified by works, affright those from allowing any place for them." Ibid.

41. Ibid., p. 455.

42. Ibid.

43. Ibid.

44. Ibid., pp. 455-57.

45. *Works:* "Witness of the Spirit," 5:120.

46. *Works:* "Minutes of Some Late Conversations, Mon., June 25, 1744," 8:476-77.

47. John Wesley, London, Nov. 30, 1770, to Joseph Benson in *The Letters of the Rev. John Wesley,* 5:211-12.

48. *Works:* "Answers to the Rev. Mr. Church," 8:386.

7: CONCLUSION

As we have examined the doctrines foundational to assurance, we have seen great disparity between the views of John Wesley and Charles Stanley. They can't both be right. The conclusion is that Wesley's theology is more consistent with the Bible and classical Christianity. By avoiding extremes on either side, he has guided us to more correct conclusions regarding the believer's security. We *can* have a confident assurance that we belong to God, but this assurance must be rooted in genuine saving faith.

Stanley's view of unconditional eternal security has some serious practical implications. It is one thing to teach that every true Christian will persevere in faith and holiness (as many Calvinists do); it is another thing to teach that every true Christian will persevere in his salvation whether or not he perseveres in faith and holiness. Stanley's adherence to the latter position avoids some of the problems of the first position—such as: Can someone really have the assurance that he is saved since he doesn't know for sure whether he will persevere in holiness? or, What about the many Christians who had real evidence of true regeneration and who later fell away, never to return to God?—but does not avoid the very serious problem of antinomianism. Stanley's view of unconditional eternal security, in which sin is harmful but no longer deadly (as far as eternity goes), is leading many into theoretical and practical antinomianism, despite Stanley's claim that his view of rewards eliminates this tendency.

More specifically, we can talk about the practical implications of Stanley's view of repentance. John Wesley believed that repentance from sin occurs *before* salvation. Stanley believes repentance from sin occurs *after* salvation. If Wesley is right, many who accept Stanley's view and refuse to repent of sin before "accepting" Christ could experience a spurious conversion and become just as deceived about their relationship with Christ as those who think good works will get them into heaven.

Much of the difference between Stanley and Wesley stems from different views of grace. Though Stanley and Wesley agree that grace is the unmerited favor of God to man, only Wesley spoke of grace as the enabling power of God working in one's heart to bring him to repentance, faith, and salvation (which includes regeneration and sanctification). For Wesley, it is this enabling grace that produces good works in a Christian. It is the fruit of this grace that will be rewarded. Since it is grace that produces the good works, God will still get all the glory even as He rewards His servants.

Stanley has some ideas in common with the Calvinists. One is related to the Calvinists' belief that salvation is completely God's responsibility. According to this teaching, man doesn't decide whether or not he will receive Christ. God determines who will be saved and who will not be saved. God then regenerates those he would save and causes them to repent and believe. All of this is God's responsibility. Man does not make the choice either to become a child of God or to remain a child of God. Calvinists think that only this view gives God all the glory for our salvation, since with this view we cannot take any credit whatsoever for our salvation. For man to be responsible for his salvation in any sense somehow undermines the sovereignty and the glory of God.

Stanley agrees with the Calvinists' view of man's responsibility, but only in respect to *maintaining* salvation, not in respect to *obtaining* salvation. Man is responsible for trusting Christ; the choice is his. God desires that all be saved, but only those who decide to trust Christ will be saved. Stanley doesn't have a problem with man being responsible for *getting* saved; he simply has a problem with man being responsible for *staying* saved. But what is the difference? If man is responsible for *entering into* a relationship with God, why shouldn't he be responsible for *continuing in* a relationship with God? If Stanley thinks that man being responsible for his salvation is "works" salvation, then he should become a full Calvinist and deny that man is responsible for even receiving salvation.

Wesley has the more Scriptural approach. It is God's grace that enables someone to respond to God's call to salvation. Man is responsible for responding, and is able to resist, but it is only through prevenient grace (John 1:9, Titus 2:11) that man's will is free enough to respond; therefore, God gets all the credit. For man to be responsible for salvation is some sense does not undermine God's sovereignty, since God sovereignly decreed that the elect are those who seek the righteousness of God by faith (see Romans 9:30-32). God has predetermined that we (as humans made in the image of God) would freely decide by grace whether or not to live in a love relationship with God.

It seems that Charles Stanley was convinced of his belief in eternal security because of an imbalanced view of the nature of God's love, the atonement, justification by faith, the law, and the whole issue of man's responsibility vs. God's responsibility. Add to this Stanley's own experience of "insecurity" and his own desire for assurance. Once Stanley was convinced of the "truth" of eternal security, he began to modify other doctrines to reconcile them to unconditional eternal security. He started teaching that sin is not what keeps one out of heaven, that repentance from sin is not necessary for salvation, that salvation stands independently of faith, and that "outer darkness" does not refer to eternal punishment, but to a lower rank in the kingdom of God. These positions and others were taken when this very intelligent man tried to use the data of Scripture to reconcile biblical doctrine to sectarian dogma.

What is the end result of Stanley's doctrine? It is giving false comfort to thousands who walk in darkness but claim to know God. Stanley is convincing souls who are lost in sin that a moment of faith has assured them of heaven forever. Many who accept Stanley's false doctrine will find themselves shut out of the kingdom to their surprise and horror. Jesus said,

> Not everyone who says to Me, "Lord, Lord," will enter the kingdom of heaven, but he who does the will of My Father in heaven. Many will say to Me in that day, "Lord, Lord, have we not proph-

esied in Your name?..." And then I will declare to them, "I never knew you; depart from Me, you who practice lawlessness!"(Matthew 7:21-23, NKJ).

Let us pray that Charles Stanley will abandon his erroneous teaching and instead declare with Scripture that "he that saith, 'I know him,' and keepeth not His commandments is a liar and the truth is not in him" (1 John 2:4).

If we are Christians, we have the awesome privilege of knowing that we are children of God. Let us reject any false hope, and rest confidently in Christ, having assurance of our salvation as long as we keep His Word (I John 2:5).

APPENDIX
WHAT THE NEW TESTAMENT TEACHES ABOUT
THE BELIEVER'S SECURITY

What does the New Testament teach about the believer's security? The following presentation will take you through the New Testament, book by book, identifying passages that relate to the issue. Persons holding different views have used many of these passages to try to prove their positions. Rather than choosing a few proof texts for support, this lists practically all the passages that seem to relate to security (parallel passages aren't necessarily repeated) and offers a simple commentary that summarizes each passage's point.

Matthew

For if ye forgive men their trespasses, your heavenly Father will also forgive you: But if ye forgive not men their trespasses, neither will your Father forgive your trespasses (6:14-15).

Our forgiveness is contingent on our forgiving others. We stand condemned if we are not forgiven.

And the brother shall deliver up the brother to death, and the father the child: and the children shall rise up against their parents, and cause them to be put to death. And ye shall be hated of all men for my name's sake: but he that endureth to the end shall be saved (10:21-22). [See also Mark 13:12-13.]

There will be pressures to deny Christ in the last days, but those that are true to the end of their lives (some experiencing martyrdom), will obtain eternal salvation. Those who fail to endure will not be saved.

And when he sowed, some seeds fell by the way side, and the fowls came and devoured them up: Some fell upon stony places, where they had not much earth: and forthwith they sprung up, because they had no deepness of earth: And when the sun was up, they were scorched; and because they had no root, they withered away... Yet hath he [the one represented by the seeds that fell on stony ground] not root in himself, but dureth for a while: for when tribulation or persecution ariseth because of the word, by and by he is offended. {offended: he relapseth, or, falleth into sin} (13:4–6, 21). [See also Mark 4:2-17.]

> *The soil represents people's hearts. Some hearts receive the gospel but do not get established. These people are saved for a time, but turn from God during temptation or persecution. It would be hard to suggest they were not saved because the text says that they did endure for a while. It would also be hard to suggest that they stayed saved—because the text says that they withered away.*

Therefore is the kingdom of heaven likened unto a certain king, which would take account of his servants. And when he had begun to reckon, one was brought unto him, which owed him ten thousand talents. But forasmuch as he had not to pay, his lord commanded him to be sold, and his wife, and children, and all that he had, and payment to be made. The servant therefore fell down, and worshipped him, saying, Lord, have patience with me, and I will pay thee all. Then the lord of that servant was moved with compassion, and loosed him, and forgave him the debt. But the same servant went out, and found one of his fellowservants, which owed him an hundred pence: and he laid hands on him, and took him by the throat, saying, Pay me that thou owest. And his fellowservant fell down at his feet, and besought him, saying, Have patience with me, and I will pay thee all. And he would not: but went and cast him into prison, till he should pay the debt. So when his fellowservants saw what was done, they were very sorry, and came and told unto their lord all that was done. Then his lord, after that he had called him, said unto him, O thou wicked servant, I forgave thee all that debt, because thou desiredst me: Shouldest not thou also have had compassion on thy fellowservant, even as I had pity on thee? And his lord was wroth, and delivered him to the tormentors, till he should pay all that was due unto him. So likewise shall my heavenly Father do also unto you, if ye from your hearts forgive not every one his brother their trespasses (18:23-35).

Jesus teaches that one could be forgiven for his sins (saved) yet forfeit that forgiveness (and thus salvation) by refusing to forgive those that offend him. One's debt of sin would be reinstated.

And then shall many be offended, and shall betray one another, and shall hate one another. And many false prophets shall rise, and shall deceive many. And because iniquity shall abound, the love of many shall wax cold. But he that shall endure unto the end, the same shall be saved (24:10-13). [See also Luke 21:7-19.]

Spiritual perseverance is necessary for eternal salvation. "Enduring to the end" must refer to spiritual perseverance because the context speaks of the deception and growing sinfulness that could influence people to reject their faith.

Therefore be ye also ready: for in such an hour as ye think not the Son of man cometh. Who then is a faithful and wise servant, whom his lord hath made ruler over his household, to give them meat in due season? Blessed is that servant, whom his lord when he cometh shall find so doing. Verily I say unto you, That he shall make him ruler over all his goods. But and if that evil servant shall say in his heart, My lord delayeth his coming; And shall begin to smite his fellowservants, and to eat and drink with the drunken; The lord of that servant shall come in a day when he looketh not for him, and in an hour that he is not aware of, And shall cut him asunder, and appoint him his portion with the hypocrites: there shall be weeping and gnashing of teeth (Luke 24:44-51). [See also Luke 12:42-46.]

This warning is given to Christ's followers. The servant of God who is not faithful to the end will be cut off. He will experience the fate of the hypocrites (eternal punishment).

Then shall the kingdom of heaven be likened unto ten virgins, which took their lamps, and went forth to meet the bridegroom. And five of them were wise, and five were foolish. They that were foolish took their lamps, and took no oil with them: But the wise took oil in their vessels with their lamps. While the bridegroom tarried, they all slumbered and slept. And at midnight there was a cry made, Behold, the bridegroom cometh; go ye out to meet him. Then all those virgins arose, and trimmed their lamps. And the foolish said unto the wise, Give us of your oil; for our lamps are gone out. {gone out: or, going out} But the wise answered, saying, Not so; lest there be not enough for us and you: but go ye rather to them that sell, and buy for yourselves. And while they went to buy, the bridegroom came; and they that were ready went in with him to the marriage: and the door was shut. Afterward came also the other virgins, saying, Lord, Lord, open to us. But he answered and said, Verily I say unto you, I know you not. Watch therefore, for ye know neither the day nor the hour wherein the Son of man cometh (25:1-13).

The only difference between the wise and foolish virgins is that the foolish allowed their lamps to burn out. They at one time had oil in their lamps. Their lamps had been burning. Jesus teaches that Christians must continue to possess the "oil" and to keep their "lamps burning," or they will shut out of the kingdom of God.

Luke

He spake also this parable; A certain man had a fig tree planted in his vineyard; and he came and sought fruit thereon, and found none. Then said he unto the dresser of his vineyard, Behold, these three years I come seeking fruit on this fig tree, and find none: cut it down; why cumbereth it the ground? And he answering said unto him, Lord, let it alone this year also, till I shall dig about it, and dung it: And if it bear fruit, well: and if not, then after that thou shalt cut it down (13:6-9).

Jesus is teaching that, though He is patient with his followers, they must eventually bear Christian fruit or he will reject them. An application could also be made to the Jewish nation, which was eventually punished for their lack of responsiveness to God.

And he said, A certain man had two sons: And the younger of them said to his father, Father, give me the portion of goods that falleth to me. And he divided unto them his living. And not many days after the younger son gathered all together, and took his journey into a far country, and there wasted his substance with riotous living. And when he had spent all, there arose a mighty famine in that land; and he began to be in want. And he went and joined himself to a citizen of that country; and he sent him into his fields to feed swine. And he would fain have filled his belly with the husks that the swine did eat: and no man gave unto him. And when he came to himself, he said, How many hired servants of my father's have bread enough and to spare, and I perish with hunger! I will arise and go to my father, and will say unto him, Father, I have sinned against heaven, and before thee, And am no more worthy to be called thy son: make me as one of thy hired servants. And he arose, and came to his father. But when he was yet a great way off, his father saw him, and had compassion, and ran, and fell on his neck, and kissed him. And the son said unto him, Father, I have sinned against heaven, and in thy sight, and am no more worthy to be called thy son. But the father said to his servants, Bring forth the best robe, and put it on him; and put a ring on his hand, and shoes on his feet: And bring hither the fatted calf, and kill it; and let us eat, and be merry: For this my son was dead, and is alive again; he was lost, and is found. And they began to be merry (15:11-24).

The point of this parable and the previous parables of the sheep and coin is about a sinner being saved, not necessarily about an erring child of God. Jesus clearly interprets the 1ˢᵗ two parables – there was great joy in heaven over one sinner being saved. Even if the parable can apply to born again Christians going astray, we must notice from verse 32 that the son was both lost and dead before he came back. Even though God loves us, we are lost and dead spiritually until we come (or come back) to the Father.

And take heed to yourselves, lest at any time your hearts be overcharged with surfeiting, and drunkenness, and cares of this life, and so that day come upon you unawares. For as a snare shall it come on all them that dwell on the face of the whole earth. Watch ye therefore, and pray always, that ye may be accounted worthy to escape all these things that shall come to pass, and to stand before the Son of man (21:34-36).

Jesus warns his followers (Christians) to take heed, lest their hearts are overcome with drunkenness and the cares of this life. Christians must watch and pray always, so that they can escape evil to come and to stand before Christ, which means to pass the judgment.

John

He that believeth on the Son hath everlasting life: and he that believeth not the Son shall not see life; but the wrath of God abideth on him (3:36).

> *The verbs in this verse are in the present tense. The one that believes and keeps on believing has everlasting life. The one who doesn't believe and keeps on in his unbelief will not see life. The wrath of God continues to abide on the unbeliever as long as he continues in his unbelief.*

Verily, verily, I say unto you, He that heareth my word, and believeth on him that sent me, hath everlasting life, and shall not come into condemnation; but is passed from death unto life (5:24).

> *The one who believes and continues to believe has eternal life and will not be condemned.*

And Jesus said unto them, I am the bread of life: he that cometh to me shall never hunger; and he that believeth on me shall never thirst (6:35).

> *The one who believes in Jesus and continues to believe will never thirst. He is continually being spiritually satisfied. Note that 'cometh' is in the present tense.*

All that the Father giveth me shall come to me; and him that cometh to me I will in no wise cast out. For I came down from heaven, not to do mine own will, but the will of him that sent me. And this is the Father's will which hath sent me, that of all which he hath given me I should lose nothing, but should raise it up again at the last day. And this is the will of him that sent me, that every one which seeth the Son, and believeth on him, may have everlasting life: and I will raise him up at the last day. (6:37-40).

> *Those whom the Father gives to the Son are those who come to Jesus in faith. Those who continually approach Christ in faith He will never cast out. Just as it is not God's will that any man perish, but that all come to repentance, so it is God's will that believers will persevere in their faith to the end. Christ will resurrect those believers.*

Then said Jesus to those Jews which believed on him, If ye continue in my word, then are ye my disciples indeed; And ye shall know the truth, and the truth shall make you free (8:31-32).

Jesus tells His followers that they must continue to love His word and keep His word to show that they were His disciples indeed.

My sheep hear my voice, and I know them, and they follow me: And I give unto them eternal life; and they shall never perish, neither shall any man pluck them out of my hand. My Father, which gave them me, is greater than all; and no man is able to pluck them out of my Father's hand (10:27-29).

True Christians hear Christ's voice and follow Him. It is to the ones who follow Jesus that He gives eternal life. I can claim God's promise to keep me if I am a true follower of Jesus.

If ye love me, keep my commandments. And I will pray the Father, and he shall give you another Comforter, that he may abide with you for ever; Even the Spirit of truth; whom the world cannot receive, because it seeth him not, neither knoweth him: but ye know him; for he dwelleth with you, and shall be in you. (14:15-17).

To those that love Him, and thus keep His commandments, Jesus promises to ask the Father to give them the Holy Spirit, who would abide forever with those that love God.

I am the true vine, and my Father is the husbandman. Every branch in me that beareth not fruit he taketh away: and every branch that beareth fruit, he purgeth it, that it may bring forth more fruit. Now ye are clean through the word which I have spoken unto you. Abide in me, and I in you. As the branch cannot bear fruit of itself, except it abide in the vine; no more can ye, except ye abide in me. I am the vine, ye are the branches: He that abideth in me, and I in him, the same bringeth forth much fruit: for without me ye can do nothing. If a man abide not in me, he is cast forth as a branch, and is withered; and men gather them, and cast them into the fire, and they are burned (15:1-6).

Christians (the branches) must be careful to abide in Christ and to bear fruit, lest God see that they have failed to abide in the vine, and He casts them away.

I pray for them: I pray not for the world, but for them which thou hast given me; for they are thine. And all mine are thine, and thine are mine; and I am glorified in them. And now I am no more in the world, but these are in the world, and I come to thee. Holy Father, keep through thine own name those whom thou hast given me, that they may be one, as we are. While I was with them in the world, I kept them in thy name: those that thou gavest me I have kept, and none of them is lost, but the son of perdition; that the scripture might be fulfilled But now I come to You, and these things I speak in the world, that they may have My joy fulfilled in themselves. "I have given them Your word; and the world has hated them because they are not of the world, just as I am not of the world. I do not pray that You should take them out of the world, but that You should keep them from the evil one....I do not pray for these alone, but also for those who will believe in Me through their word; that they all may be one, as You, Father, are in Me, and I in You; that they also may be one in Us, that the world may believe that You sent Me. And the glory which You gave Me I have given them, that they may be one just as We are one: I in them, and You in Me; that they may be made perfect in one, and that the world may know that You have sent Me, and have loved them as You have loved Me. Father, I desire that they also whom You gave Me may be with Me where I am, that they may behold My glory which You have given Me; for You loved Me before the foundation of the world (17:9-24).

Jesus prays for those who were believing in Him during his earthly ministry, and for those who later would be believing in Him, that they would be one, that they may be perfect, and that they may come to be with Him so that they could see His glory. The prayer would be answered because sufficient grace would be extended to all those who sought to fulfill these purposes.

Acts

And as many as were ordained to eternal life believed (13:48b).

Those Gentiles who believed were those whom God foreknew would respond by turning away from sin and toward Christ. There is no guarantee in this verse that those Gentiles would continue in their faith.

Take heed therefore unto yourselves, and to all the flock, over the which the Holy Ghost hath made you overseers, to feed the church of God, which he hath purchased with his own blood. For I know this, that after my departing shall grievous wolves enter in among you, not sparing the flock. Also of your own selves shall men arise, speaking perverse things, to draw away disciples after them. Therefore watch, and remember, that by the space of three years I ceased not to warn every one night and day (20:28-31).

Paul warns the Christians that evil people will try to draw them away from Christ. This shows that the danger is real even for true believers.

Romans

And thinkest thou this, O man, that judgest them which do such things, and doest the same, that thou shalt escape the judgment of God? Or despisest thou the riches of his goodness and forbearance and longsuffering; not knowing that the goodness of God leadeth thee to repentance? But after thy hardness and impenitent heart treasurest up unto thyself wrath against the day of wrath and revelation of the righteous judgment of God; Who will render to every man according to his deeds: To them who by patient continuance in well doing seek for glory and honour and immortality, eternal life: But unto them that are contentious, and do not obey the truth, but obey unrighteousness, indignation and wrath (2:3-8).

Eternal life comes to those who patiently continue to do good. If one doesn't obey the truth, he will experience judgment.

What then? Shall we sin, because we are not under the law, but under grace? God forbid. Know ye not, that to whom ye yield yourselves servants to obey, his servants ye are to whom ye obey; whether of sin unto death, or of obedience unto righteousness? (6:15-16).

Whether or not we at one time had entered into a real relationship with Christ, our obedience or disobedience will determine whether we live or die spiritually. Death means judgment in Romans.

But now being made free from sin, and become servants to God, ye have your fruit unto holiness, and the end everlasting life. For the wages of sin is death; but the gift of God is eternal life through Jesus Christ our Lord. (6:22-23).

The end of a holy life is eternal life, the gift of God.

So, then, brethren, we are debtors, not to the flesh, to live according to the flesh; for if according to the flesh ye do live, ye are about to die; and if, by the Spirit, the deeds of the body ye put to death, ye shall live (8:12-13).

Spiritual life is conditioned upon putting to death the deeds of the body. Note that Paul addresses his audience as brethren. They had spiritual life; in order for them to continue to have spiritual life they needed to continue to be dead to the deeds of the flesh.

For whom He foreknew, He also predestined to be conformed to the image of His Son, that He might be the firstborn among many brethren (8:29).

Those whom God foreknew would believe and keep on believing in Him, He determined that He would conform to the image of Christ. There is no unconditional guarantee of security promised in this passage or the next.

Moreover whom he did predestinate, them he also called: and whom he called, them he also justified: and whom he justified, them he also glorified (8:30).

Paul is telling the process through which God takes all who are elect in Christ – He calls them, he justifies them, and glorifies them.

All things work together for good to them that love God....What shall we then say to these things? If God be for us, who can be against us? He that spared not his own Son, but delivered him up for us all, how shall he not with him also freely give us all things? Who shall lay any thing to the charge of God's elect? It is God that justifieth. Who is he that condemneth? It is Christ that died, yea rather, that is risen again, who is even at the right hand of God, who also maketh intercession for us. Who shall separate us from the love of Christ? shall tribulation, or distress, or persecution, or famine, or nakedness, or peril, or sword? As it is written, For thy sake we are killed all the day long; we are accounted as sheep for the slaughter. Nay, in all these things we are more than conquerors through him that loved us.

For I am persuaded, that neither death, nor life, nor angels, nor principalities, nor powers, nor things present, nor things to come, Nor height, nor depth, nor any other creature, shall be able to separate us from the love of God, which is in Christ Jesus our Lord. (8:28a, 8:31-39).

> *True believers (those who are presently loving God) are the "us" in this passage. Those believers stand uncondemned. Christ makes intercession for them. God will give them freely all things. Nothing can separate these true believers from the love of God. There is no unconditional guarantee of security promised in this passage.*

Therefore hath he mercy on whom he will have mercy, and whom he will he hardeneth. Thou wilt say then unto me, Why doth he yet find fault? For who hath resisted his will? Nay but, O man, who art thou that repliest against God? Shall the thing formed say to him that formed it, Why hast thou made me thus? Hath not the potter power over the clay, of the same lump to make one vessel unto honour, and another unto dishonour? What if God, willing to shew his wrath, and to make his power known, endured with much longsuffering the vessels of wrath fitted to destruction: And that he might make known the riches of his glory on the vessels of mercy, which he had afore prepared unto glory, Even us, whom he hath called, not of the Jews only, but also of the Gentiles? As he saith also in Osee, I will call them my people, which were not my people; and her beloved, which was not beloved. And it shall come to pass, that in the place where it was said unto them, Ye are not my people; there shall they be called the children of the living God. Esaias also crieth concerning Israel, Though the number of the children of Israel be as the sand of the sea, a remnant shall be saved: For he will finish the work, and cut it short in righteousness: because a short work will the Lord make upon the earth. And as Esaias said before, Except the Lord of Sabaoth had left us a seed, we had been as Sodoma, and been made like unto Gomorrha. What shall we say then? That the Gentiles, which followed not after righteousness, have attained to righteousness, even the righteousness which is of faith. But Israel, which followed after the law of righteousness, hath not attained to the law of righteousness. Wherefore? Because they sought it not by faith, but as it were by the works of the law. For they stumbled at that stumblingstone; As it is written, Behold, I lay in Sion a stumblingstone and rock of offence: and whosoever believeth on him shall not be ashamed (9:18-32).

Paul says in this passage that God has the right to choose people for salvation on any basis he wishes; after all, He is God, the Creator. On what basis, then, has he determined to save people, making them "vessels of mercy"? According to the last part of this passage, God chooses to save those who seek the righteousness of God by faith.

For I speak to you Gentiles, inasmuch as I am the apostle of the Gentiles, I magnify mine office: If by any means I may provoke to emulation them which are my flesh, and might save some of them. For if the casting away of them be the reconciling of the world, what shall the receiving of them be, but life from the dead? For if the firstfruit be holy, the lump is also holy: and if the root be holy, so are the branches. And if some of the branches be broken off, and thou, being a wild olive tree, wert graffed in among them, and with them partakest of the root and fatness of the olive tree; Boast not against the branches. But if thou boast, thou bearest not the root, but the root thee. Thou wilt say then, The branches were broken off, that I might be graffed in. Well; because of unbelief they were broken off, and thou standest by faith. Be not highminded, but fear: For if God spared not the natural branches, take heed lest he also spare not thee. Behold therefore the goodness and severity of God: on them which fell, severity; but toward thee, goodness, if thou continue in his goodness: otherwise thou also shalt be cut off. And they also, if they abide not still in unbelief, shall be graffed in: for God is able to graff them in again (11:13-23).

The Jews were clearly in the "tree," but just as the Jews were cut off because of unbelief, we as individual Christians will be cut off if we don't continue faithfully in God's goodness. We stand in the grace of God by faith. We should fear God, knowing that we will be cut off if we don't continue in the faith. Note that verse 23 says that the Jews can be grafted back in again – backsliding is not permanent.

As concerning the gospel, they are enemies for your sakes: but as touching the election, they are beloved for the fathers' sakes. For the gifts and calling of God are without repentance. For as ye in times past have not believed God, yet have now obtained mercy through their unbelief: Even so have these also now not believed, that through your mercy they also may obtain mercy (11:28-31).

The Jews are loved by God with a special love, because of the promises made to the fathers, including Abraham, Jacob, and David. God had called the Jews for a special purpose, and He will not change His mind about that. All of humanity can receive mercy because of the people of Israel. Christ came to all humanity through the Jewish nation. This passage really doesn't speak to the issue of assurance or security.

Now to him that is of power to stablish you according to my gospel, and the preaching of Jesus Christ, according to the revelation of the mystery, which was kept secret since the world began, But now is made manifest, and by the scriptures of the prophets, according to the commandment of the everlasting God, made known to all nations for the obedience of faith: To God only wise, be glory through Jesus Christ for ever. Amen (16:25-27).

God is able to establish us in his grace, by the revelation of Jesus Christ.

I Corinthians

Know ye not that they which run in a race run all, but one receiveth the prize? So run, that ye may obtain. And every man that striveth for the mastery is temperate in all things. Now they do it to obtain a corruptible crown; but we an incorruptible. I therefore so run, not as uncertainly; so fight I, not as one that beateth the air: But I keep under my body, and bring it into subjection: lest that by any means, when I have preached to others, I myself should be a castaway (9:24-27).

Even Paul would be a castaway (rejected by God the Judge) if he did not bring his body into subjection.

Now these things were our examples, to the intent we should not lust after evil things, as they also lusted. Neither be ye idolaters, as were some of them; as it is written, The people sat down to eat and drink, and rose up to play. Neither let us commit fornication, as some of them committed, and fell in one day three and twenty thousand.

Neither let us tempt Christ, as some of them also tempted, and were destroyed of serpents. Neither murmur ye, as some of them also murmured, and were destroyed of the destroyer. Now all these things happened unto them for ensamples: and they are written for our admonition, upon whom the ends of the world are come. Wherefore let him that thinketh he standeth take heed lest he fall. There hath no temptation taken you but such as is common to man: but God is faithful, who will not suffer you to be tempted above that ye are able; but will with the temptation also make a way to escape, that ye may be able to bear it. Wherefore, my dearly beloved, flee from idolatry (10:6-14).

If we think we are secure, we need to take heed, because temptation could overtake us if we are not on our guard. We are warned not to be like the Israelites, who died for their sins. Fortunately, we have a promise from God – He provides a way of escape from temptation.

II Corinthians

Now he that hath wrought us for the selfsame thing is God, who also hath given unto us the earnest of the Spirit. Therefore we are always confident, knowing that, whilst we are at home in the body, we are absent from the Lord: (For we walk by faith, not by sight:) We are confident, I say, and willing rather to be absent from the body, and to be present with the Lord. Wherefore we labour, that, whether present or absent, we may be accepted of him. For we must all appear before the judgment seat of Christ; that every one may receive the things done in his body, according to that he hath done, whether it be good or bad. Knowing therefore the terror of the Lord, we persuade men; but we are made manifest unto God; and I trust also are made manifest in your consciences (5:5-11).

God the Father has given us the Spirit as a guarantee of our inheritance. As long as we have Him, we are secure. Because we have the Spirit, we are always confident that if we were to die, we would go to be with Jesus. Therefore we seek to be well-pleasing to God, knowing that someday we will stand before Christ at the judgment.

Examine yourselves, whether ye be in the faith; prove your own selves. Know ye not your own selves, how that Jesus Christ is in you, except ye be reprobates? But I trust that ye shall know that we are not reprobates (13:5-6).

Paul speaks of the real possibility of being disqualified, rejected, or reprobate, and no longer being in the faith.

Galatians

I marvel that ye are so soon removed from him that called you into the grace of Christ unto another gospel (1:6).

It is possible for real Christians to turn away from God and to another gospel. In fact, this happened to at least some of the Galatians.

But now, after that ye have known God, or rather are known of God, how turn ye again to the weak and beggarly elements, whereunto ye desire again to be in bondage? Ye observe days, and months, and times, and years. I am afraid of you, lest I have bestowed upon you labour in vain (4:9-11).

Paul is worrying here that the Galatians had made choices that would cause his labor among them to be in vain. It would only be in vain if they had forfeited the salvation that Paul helped them to receive.

For I testify again to every man that is circumcised, that he is a debtor to do the whole law. Christ is become of no effect unto you, whosoever of you are justified by the law; ye are fallen from grace. For we through the Spirit wait for the hope of righteousness by faith. For in Jesus Christ neither circumcision availeth any thing, nor uncircumcision; but faith which worketh by love. Ye did run well; who did hinder you that ye should not obey the truth? (5:3-7).

Only continued faith working through love avails anything. We fall from grace if we attempt to be justified by the law.

Be not deceived; God is not mocked: for whatsoever a man soweth, that shall he also reap. For he that soweth to his flesh shall of the flesh reap corruption; but he that soweth to the Spirit shall of the Spirit reap life everlasting (6:7-8).

We must be careful to sow to the Spirit in order to reap everlasting life. If we sow to our flesh we will die spiritually. We must not be deceived into thinking that we can live according to the flesh and go to heaven. God will not be mocked by that philosophy.

Ephesians

Blessed be the God and Father of our Lord Jesus Christ, who hath blessed us with all spiritual blessings in heavenly places in Christ: According as he hath chosen us in him before the foundation of the world, that we should be holy and without blame before him in love: Having predestinated us unto the adoption of children by Jesus Christ to himself, according to the good pleasure of his will, To the praise of the glory of his grace, wherein he hath made us accepted in the beloved. In whom we have redemption through his blood, the forgiveness of sins, according to the riches of his grace; Wherein he hath abounded toward us in all wisdom and prudence; Having made known unto us the mystery of his will, according to his good pleasure which he hath purposed in himself: That in the dispensation of the fulness of times he might gather together in one all things in Christ, both which are in heaven, and which are on earth; even in him: In whom also we have obtained an inheritance, being predestinated according to the purpose of him who worketh all things after the counsel of his own will: That we should be to the praise of his glory, who first trusted in Christ. In whom ye also trusted, after that ye heard the word of truth, the gospel of your salvation: in whom also after that ye believed, ye were sealed with that holy Spirit of promise, Which is the earnest of our inheritance until the redemption of the purchased possession, unto the praise of his glory. (1:3-14).

Before the foundation of the world, God determined that believers would be adopted into the family of God, become holy, and bring praise to Christ. Believers are sealed with the Holy Spirit, who is the guarantee of their inheritance. As long as we have the Holy Spirit, we are guaranteed to be ultimately redeemed.

For by grace are ye saved through faith; and that not of yourselves: it is the gift of God: Not of works, lest any man should boast. For we are his workmanship, created in Christ Jesus unto good works, which God hath before ordained that we should walk in them. (2:8-10).

We must completely rely on God's grace, knowing there is nothing we can do to deserve salvation. It is by God's grace that we are saved and enabled to produce the good works that inevitably flow from a true relationship with God.

Let no corrupt communication proceed out of your mouth, but that which is good to the use of edifying, that it may minister grace unto the hearers. And grieve not the holy Spirit of God, whereby ye are sealed unto the day of redemption. Let all bitterness, and wrath, and anger, and clamour, and evil speaking, be put away from you, with all malice: And be ye kind one to another, tenderhearted, forgiving one another, even as God for Christ's sake hath forgiven you (4:29-32).

The Holy Spirit is our seal, signifying that we are God's property. We must not grieve the Holy Spirit (as the Israelites provoked the Holy Spirit, making Him their enemy), for only those who have the Holy Spirit have a guarantee that they will go to heaven.

But fornication, and all uncleanness, or covetousness, let it not be once named among you, as becometh saints; Neither filthiness, nor foolish talking, nor jesting, which are not convenient: but rather giving of thanks. For this ye know, that no whoremonger, nor unclean person, nor covetous man, who is an idolater, hath any inheritance in the kingdom of Christ and of God. Let no man deceive you with vain words: for because of these things cometh the wrath of God upon the children of disobedience. Be not ye therefore partakers with them (5:3-7).

Paul warns Christians not to partake in the deeds of the sons of disobedience, who commit sexual sins, who covet, and who are idolatrous. Those who do these things will not go to heaven. Don't let anyone deceive you about this. Even though you are a Christian now, if you involve yourself in these deeds you will experience the wrath of God.

Philippians

Always in every prayer of mine for you all making request with joy, For your fellowship in the gospel from the first day until now; Being confident of this very thing, that he which hath begun a good work in you will perform it until the day of Jesus Christ:Even as it is meet for me to think this of you all, because I have you in my heart; inasmuch as both in my bonds, and in the defence and confirmation of the gospel, ye all are partakers of my grace. (1:4-7).

Paul had confidence in the Philippians. Because they were partaking of grace, Paul believed that God would complete in them the work that He had started. As long as they chose to partake of grace, God would continue to work in them.

Yea doubtless, and I count all things but loss for the excellency of the knowledge of Christ Jesus my Lord: for whom I have suffered the loss of all things, and do count them but dung, that I may win Christ, And be found in him, not having mine own righteousness, which is of the law, but that which is through the faith of Christ, the righteousness which is of God by faith: That I may know him, and the power of his resurrection, and the fellowship of his sufferings, being made conformable unto his death; If by any means I might attain unto the resurrection of the dead. Not as though I had already attained, either were already perfect: but I follow after, if that I may apprehend that for which also I am apprehended of Christ Jesus. Brethren, I count not myself to have apprehended: but this one thing I do, forgetting those things which are behind, and reaching forth unto those things which are before, I press toward the mark for the prize of the high calling of God in Christ Jesus. (3:8-14).

Paul did not consider himself as having an absolutely guaranteed salvation. He pressed on in faith, so that he might attain to the resurrection from the dead. Paul himself did not think he would be raised from the dead in a glorified body without further perseverance on his part.

I Thessalonians

For this cause, when I could no longer forbear, I sent to know your faith, lest by some means the tempter have tempted you, and our labour be in vain (3:5).

Paul's labor would have been in vain had his converts succumbed to the temptations of the devil to abandon the gospel. How could his labor have been in vain if they could not have forfeited the salvation he helped them obtain?

II Thessalonians

Finally, brethren, pray for us, that the word of the Lord may have free course, and be glorified, even as it is with you: And that we may be delivered from unreasonable and wicked men: for all men have not faith. But the Lord is faithful, who shall stablish you, and keep you from evil. And we have confidence in the Lord touching you, that ye both do and will do the things which we command you. And the Lord direct your hearts into the love of God, and into the patient waiting for Christ (3:1-5).

God is faithful to establish the believer and guard him from the evil one. This promise is given to the believer who continues to do what the Bible teaches.

I Timothy

Now the end of the commandment is charity out of a pure heart, and of a good conscience, and of faith unfeigned: From which some having swerved have turned aside unto vain jangling (1:5-6).

Paul indicates that some people had strayed away from sincere faith. This of course means that they at one time had a sincere faith in Christ but no longer.

This charge I commit unto thee, son Timothy, according to the prophecies which went before on thee, that thou by them mightest war a good warfare; Holding faith, and a good conscience; which some having put away concerning faith have made shipwreck: Of whom is Hymenaeus and Alexander; whom I have delivered unto Satan, that they may learn not to blaspheme (1:18-20).

Paul names people who had made shipwreck of their faith. They at one time had a real faith, but now they were blaspheming God. This shows that making shipwreck is not only possible, but has actually happened.

Now the Spirit speaketh expressly, that in the latter times some shall depart from the faith, giving heed to seducing spirits, and doctrines of devils; Speaking lies in hypocrisy; having their conscience seared with a hot iron (4:1-2).

The Spirit expressly says that in the latter times some would depart from the faith, giving heed to deceiving spirits and doctrines of de-

mons. How can one speak any more plainly than that? One denies the word of the Spirit if he says that the believer could never depart from the faith.

Take heed unto thyself, and unto the doctrine; continue in them: for in doing this thou shalt both save thyself, and them that hear thee (4:16).

> *The only way you will be saved is by continuing in the doctrine Paul taught. You must take heed.*

But the younger widows refuse: for when they have begun to wax wanton against Christ, they will marry; Having damnation, because they have cast off their first faith (5:11-12).

> *Paul refers to some who had cast off their first faith.*

O Timothy, keep that which is committed to thy trust, avoiding profane and vain babblings, and oppositions of science falsely so called: Which some professing have erred concerning the faith. Grace be with thee. Amen (6:20-21).

> *Again Paul speaks of those who had strayed from the faith.*

II Timothy

It is a faithful saying: For if we be dead with him, we shall also live with him: If we suffer, we shall also reign with him: if we deny him, he also will deny us: If we believe not, yet he abideth faithful: he cannot deny himself (2:11-13).

> *Some would say that verse 13 teaches eternal security. But that verse simply contrasts the character of some men to the character of God. Some Christians may end up faithless, but God will be true to Himself. The previous verse indicates that if we deny Him in our faithlessness, God will deny us. We will only reign with Him if we endure to the end.*

But shun profane and vain babblings: for they will increase unto more ungodliness. And their word will eat as doth a canker: of whom is Hymenaeus and Philetus; Who concerning the truth have erred, saying that the resurrection is past already; and overthrow the faith of some. Nevertheless the foundation of God standeth sure, having this seal, The Lord knoweth them that are his. And, Let every one that nameth the name of Christ depart from iniquity (2:16-19).

> *Paul mentions the leaders who strayed from the truth and then overthrew the true faith of some others. Unfortunately, true believers can be deceived if they are not careful.*

Hebrews

And Moses verily was faithful in all his house, as a servant, for a testimony of those things which were to be spoken after; But Christ as a son over his own house; whose house are we, if we hold fast the confidence and the rejoicing of the hope firm unto the end. Wherefore (as the Holy Ghost saith, To day if ye will hear his voice, Harden not your hearts, as in the provocation, in the day of temptation in the wilderness: When your fathers tempted me, proved me, and saw my works forty years. Wherefore I was grieved with that generation, and said, They do alway err in their heart; and they have not known my ways. So I sware in my wrath, They shall not enter into my rest.) Take heed, brethren, lest there be in any of you an evil heart of unbelief, in departing from the living God. But exhort one another daily, while it is called To day; lest any of you be hardened through the deceitfulness of sin. For we are made partakers of Christ, if we hold the beginning of our confidence stedfast unto the end (3:5-14).

> *This whole passage encourages us to keep our confidence in Christ to the end so that we will experience ultimate salvation. We must beware lest any of us depart from God. We must exhort each other daily, so our hearts are not hardened through the deceitfulness of sin. We must not stray, lest we experience judgment like the rebellious Israelites did. The possibility of departing from God must be real; otherwise, why would Paul exhort us to persevere, especially in such serious tones?*

Therefore leaving the principles of the doctrine of Christ, let us go on unto perfection; not laying again the foundation of repentance from dead works, and of faith toward God, Of the doctrine of baptisms, and of laying on of hands, and of resurrection of the dead, and of eternal judgment. And this will we do, if God permit. For it is impossible for those who were once enlightened, and have tasted of the heavenly gift, and were made partakers of the Holy Ghost, And have tasted the good word of God, and the powers of the world to come, If they shall fall away, to renew them again unto repentance; seeing they crucify to themselves the Son of God afresh, and put him to an open shame. For the earth which drinketh in the rain that cometh oft upon it, and bringeth forth herbs meet for them by whom it is dressed, receiveth blessing from God: But that which beareth thorns and briers is rejected, and is nigh unto cursing; whose end is to be burned. But, beloved, we are persuaded better things of you, and things that accompany salvation, though we thus speak. For God is not unrighteous to forget your work and labour of love, which ye have shewed toward his name, in that ye have ministered to the saints, and do minister. And we desire that every one of you do shew the same diligence to the full assurance of hope unto the end: That ye be not slothful, but followers of them who through faith and patience inherit the promises (6:1-12).

> *We must go on to perfection because we don't want to fall away. If one does fall away from salvation, it is impossible for him to repent as long as he is crucifying again the Son of God and putting Him to an open shame. God will reject those who reject Him. But the Hebrews writer was optimistic about the perseverance of his audience, since there was great evidence of their faithfulness. However, we must make sure that we show the same diligence he saw in them, and through faith and patience inherit the promise of Heaven.*

And they truly were many priests, because they were not suffered to continue by reason of death: But this man, because he continueth ever, hath an unchangeable priesthood. Wherefore he is able also to save them to the uttermost that come unto God by him, seeing he ever liveth to make intercession for them (7:23-25).

> *Jesus saves completely and forever those who are coming to Him, because He always lives to make intercession for those who are responding to Him.*

But this man, after he had offered one sacrifice for sins for ever, sat down on the right hand of God; From henceforth expecting till his enemies be made his footstool. For by one offering he hath perfected for ever them that are sanctified (10:12-14).

> *Jesus' death on the cross was sufficient to provide full and forever cleansing for all who are willing to be made holy. Those whom He*

*makes holy can be sanctified forever because of the once-for-all of-
fering of Jesus. No other sacrifice is necessary.*

Let us hold fast the profession of our faith without wavering; (for
he is faithful that promised;) And let us consider one another to provoke unto love and to good works: Not forsaking the assembling of
ourselves together, as the manner of some is; but exhorting one another: and so much the more, as ye see the day approaching. For if
we sin wilfully after that we have received the knowledge of the
truth, there remaineth no more sacrifice for sins, But a certain fearful
looking for of judgment and fiery indignation, which shall devour
the adversaries. He that despised Moses' law died without mercy
under two or three witnesses: Of how much sorer punishment, sup-
pose ye, shall he be thought worthy, who hath trodden under foot the
Son of God, and hath counted the blood of the covenant, wherewith
he was sanctified, an unholy thing, and hath done despite unto the
Spirit of grace? For we know him that hath said, Vengeance belongeth
unto me, I will recompense, saith the Lord. And again, The Lord
shall judge his people. It is a fearful thing to fall into the hands of the
living God (10:23-31).

*The author of Hebrews argues that we must not consider ourselves
unconditionally secure in Christ. We must have fellowship with other
believers to encourage each other to persevere in the faith. Why?
Because we must not willfully sin against God. Those who do can
look forward to the judgment of God. If we who have been sanctified
show blatant disrespect for the work of Christ, insulting the Spirit of
grace, God will destroy us. We should be afraid of being punished by
God.*

Cast not away therefore your confidence, which hath great recompense of reward. For ye have need of patience, that, after ye have
done the will of God, ye might receive the promise. For yet a little
while, and he that shall come will come, and will not tarry. Now the
just shall live by faith: but if any man draw back, my soul shall have
no pleasure in him. But we are not of them who draw back unto
perdition; but of them that believe to the saving of the soul (10:35-
39).

*We must not cast away our confidence in Christ. We must endure in
our faith. If we draw back from faith, we draw back to perdition.*

Wherefore seeing we also are compassed about with so great a cloud of witnesses, let us lay aside every weight, and the sin which doth so easily beset us, and let us run with patience the race that is set before us, Looking unto Jesus the author and finisher of our faith; who for the joy that was set before him endured the cross, despising the shame, and is set down at the right hand of the throne of God (12:1-2).

We must run with endurance, looking to Jesus, the one who initiates and perfects the faith that we have. As long as we run with endurance, keeping our confidence in Christ, we are secure in Him.

If ye endure chastening, God dealeth with you as with sons; for what son is he whom the father chasteneth not? But if ye be without chastisement, whereof all are partakers, then are ye bastards, and not sons. Furthermore we have had fathers of our flesh which corrected us, and we gave them reverence: shall we not much rather be in subjection unto the Father of spirits, and live? (12:7-9).

When our heavenly Father chastens us (and He will, for He loves us), we must submit to Him in order to continue to live spiritually.

Follow peace with all men, and holiness, without which no man shall see the Lord: Looking diligently lest any man fail of the grace of God; lest any root of bitterness springing up trouble you, and thereby many be defiled (12:14-15).

We must be careful not to fall short of the grace of God, become bitter, and defile others.

Let your conversation be without covetousness; and be content with such things as ye have: for he hath said, I will never leave thee, nor forsake thee. So that we may boldly say, The Lord is my helper, and I will not fear what man shall do unto me (13:5-6).

The true believer doesn't need to worry about his needs. God will not forsake the true believer. God will help and protect.

James

Brethren, if any of you do err from the truth, and one convert him; Let him know, that he which converteth the sinner from the error of his way shall save a soul from death, and shall hide a multitude of sins (5:19-20).

If someone converts a brother who wanders from the truth of the gospel, he is saving a soul from spiritual death.

I Peter

Blessed be the God and Father of our Lord Jesus Christ, which according to his abundant mercy hath begotten us again unto a lively hope by the resurrection of Jesus Christ from the dead, To an inheritance incorruptible, and undefiled, and that fadeth not away, reserved in heaven for you, Who are kept by the power of God through faith unto salvation ready to be revealed in the last time (1:3-5).

We are kept by the power of God through (continual) faith. Without faith there is no power and no keeping.

II Peter

And beside this, giving all diligence, add to your faith virtue; and to virtue knowledge; And to knowledge temperance; and to temperance patience; and to patience godliness; And to godliness brotherly kindness; and to brotherly kindness charity. For if these things be in you, and abound, they make you that ye shall neither be barren nor unfruitful in the knowledge of our Lord Jesus Christ. But he that lacketh these things is blind, and cannot see afar off, and hath forgotten that he was purged from his old sins. Wherefore the rather, brethren, give diligence to make your calling and election sure: for if ye do these things, ye shall never fall: For so an entrance shall be ministered unto you abundantly into the everlasting kingdom of our Lord and Saviour Jesus Christ (1:5-11).

We must be diligent to make our calling and election sure, not forgetting that we were cleansed from our old sins. We must add to our faith virtue, knowledge, self-control, perseverance, godliness, brotherly kindness, and love, so that we won't stumble but instead have an abundant entrance into the everlasting kingdom of Christ.

For if after they have escaped the pollutions of the world through the knowledge of the Lord and Saviour Jesus Christ, they are again entangled therein, and overcome, the latter end is worse with them than the beginning. For it had been better for them not to have known the way of righteousness, than, after they have known it, to turn from the holy commandment delivered unto them. But it is happened unto them according to the true proverb, The dog is turned to his own vomit again; and the sow that was washed to her wallowing in the mire (2:20-22).

If someone comes to truly know the Lord, then turns away, he would be better off never having been a Christian.

And account that the longsuffering of our Lord is salvation; even as our beloved brother Paul also according to the wisdom given unto him hath written unto you; As also in all his epistles, speaking in them of these things; in which are some things hard to be understood, which they that are unlearned and unstable wrest, as they do also the other scriptures, unto their own destruction. Ye therefore, beloved, seeing ye know these things before, beware lest ye also, being led away with the error of the wicked, fall from your own stedfastness. But grow in grace, and in the knowledge of our Lord and Saviour Jesus Christ. To him be glory both now and for ever. Amen (3:15-18).

Peter warns his readers to beware lest they fall from their steadfastness, and are led away with the error of the wicked. Instead, they are to grow in grace. These verses teach that Christians can choose to grow in the Lord, or they can fail to be careful enough to avoid spiritual failure.

I John

If we say that we have fellowship with him, and walk in darkness, we lie, and do not the truth: But if we walk in the light, as he is in the light, we have fellowship one with another, and the blood of Jesus Christ his Son cleanseth us from all sin (1:6-7).

If we say we are born of God but live in sin, we are liars. Experiencing communion with God and cleansing from all sin is conditioned upon walking in the light, obeying what God commands.

And hereby we do know that we know him, if we keep his commandments. He that saith, I know him, and keepeth not his commandments, is a liar, and the truth is not in him. But whoso keepeth his word, in him verily is the love of God perfected: hereby know we that we are in him. He that saith he abideth in him ought himself also so to walk, even as he walked (2:3-6).

We can have no assurance without keeping God's commands. That's how we know we are true Christians—if we walk as he walked.

Little children, it is the last time: and as ye have heard that antichrist shall come, even now are there many antichrists; whereby we know that it is the last time. They went out from us, but they were not of us; for if they had been of us, they would no doubt have continued with us: but they went out, that they might be made manifest that they were not all of us (2:18-19).

The antichrists that John refers to did not continue to identify with true Christianity because they were not true Christians. God made sure that, in their case, they were revealed for who they really were. The antichrists were not allowed to remain "tares among the wheat."

Let that therefore abide in you, which ye have heard from the beginning. If that which ye have heard from the beginning shall remain in you, ye also shall continue in the Son, and in the Father. And this is the promise that he hath promised us, even eternal life (2:24-26).

We must continue in the teaching that was delivered to us, in order to continue in the Son and Father. If we do, we have eternal life.

Little children, let no man deceive you: he that doeth righteousness is righteous, even as he is righteous. He that committeth sin is of the devil; for the devil sinneth from the beginning. For this purpose the Son of God was manifested, that he might destroy the works of the devil. Whosoever is born of God doth not commit sin; for his seed remaineth in him: and he cannot sin, because he is born of God. In this the children of God are manifest, and the children of the devil: whosoever doeth not righteousness is not of God, neither he that loveth not his brother (3:7-10).

Don't let anyone deceive you into thinking that you can live a sinful life and still be a real Christian. Christ came to destroy sin; therefore all who are Christ's do not live in willful sin. They cannot live in sin as long as "His seed" remains in them. The difference between a child of God and a child of the devil is that the child of God doesn't persist in willful sin; the child of Satan does.

My little children, let us not love in word, neither in tongue; but in deed and in truth. And hereby we know that we are of the truth, and shall assure our hearts before him. For if our heart condemn us, God is greater than our heart, and knoweth all things. Beloved, if our heart condemn us not, then have we confidence toward God. And whatsoever we ask, we receive of him, because we keep his commandments, and do those things that are pleasing in his sight. (3:18-22).

We can have a present assurance that we are born of God if our heart doesn't condemn us. Our hearts won't condemn us if we keep God's commands, doing what is pleasing to Him, loving others in deed and truth.

These things have I written unto you that believe on the name of the Son of God; that ye may know that ye have eternal life, and that ye may believe on the name of the Son of God (5:13).

We can have an assurance that we have eternal life as long as we continue to believe in Jesus.

II John

For many deceivers are entered into the world, who confess not that Jesus Christ is come in the flesh. This is a deceiver and an antichrist. Look to yourselves, that we lose not those things which we have wrought, but that we receive a full reward (1:7-8).

John warns his readers to look to themselves spiritually so that his work would not be in vain.

Jude

But ye, beloved, building up yourselves on your most holy faith, praying in the Holy Ghost, Keep yourselves in the love of God, looking for the mercy of our Lord Jesus Christ unto eternal life. And of some have compassion, making a difference: And others save with fear, pulling them out of the fire; hating even the garment spotted by the flesh. Now unto him that is able to keep you from falling, and to present you faultless before the presence of his glory with exceeding joy (20-24).

With God's help, we are to keep ourselves in the love of God, so that we don't stumble or fall. We must not only watch over ourselves but over others as well, with some taking drastic measures to keep them from the fires of sin (and potentially the fires of Hell). God has the power to keep all of us from falling and to present us faultless before His throne.

Revelation

Nevertheless I have somewhat against thee, because thou hast left thy first love. Remember therefore from whence thou art fallen, and repent, and do the first works; or else I will come unto thee quickly, and will remove thy candlestick out of his place, except thou repent (2:4-5).

The Ephesians were given a space to repent (and return to their first love) before their lampstand would be removed from its place.

Be thou faithful unto death, and I will give thee a crown of life. He that hath an ear, let him hear what the Spirit saith unto the churches; He that overcometh shall not be hurt of the second death (2:10b-11).

We must be an overcomer in order to escape the second death.

He that overcometh, the same shall be clothed in white raiment; and I will not blot out his name out of the book of life, but I will confess his name before my Father, and before his angels (3:5).

The overcomer's name will not be blotted out of the Book of Life. This implies that the name of the one who doesn't overcome will be blotted out of the Book of Life.

The beast that thou sawest was, and is not; and shall ascend out of the bottomless pit, and go into perdition: and they that dwell on the earth shall wonder, whose names were not written in the book of life from the foundation of the world, when they behold the beast that was, and is not, and yet is (17:8).

From the beginning of the world until now, God has been writing names into the Book of Life. John refers to people whose names were not in this Book.

For I testify unto every man that heareth the words of the prophecy of this book, If any man shall add unto these things, God shall add unto him the plagues that are written in this book: And if any man shall take away from the words of the book of this prophecy, God shall take away his part out of the book of life, and out of the holy city, and from the things which are written in this book (22:18-19).

> *If someone takes away from the book of Revelation, God will take away his part from the Book of Life. This implies that someone could have a part in the Book of Life, but then forfeit that part.*

BIBLIOGRAPHY

Primary Sources

Burwash, Rev. S.T.D. *Wesley's Doctrinal Standards.* Salem, OH: Schmul Pub., 1988.

Jackson, Thomas, ed. *The Works of the Rev. John Wesley, A.M.;* with the Last Corrections of the Author. 3rd ed., 14 vols.; London: Wesleyan-Methodist Book-Room, 1829-31.

Osborne, G., collector. *The Poetical Works of John and Charles Wesley.* 13 vols. London: Wesleyan-Methodist Conference Office, 1868-72.

Stanley, Charles. *Eternal Security, Can You Be Sure?* Nashville: Thomas Nelson, 1990.

——. *The Wonderful Spirit-Filled Life.* Nashville: Thomas Nelson, 1992.

Telford, John, ed. *The Letters of the Rev. John Wesley, A. M.* London: The Epworth Press, 1931.

Wesley, John. *A Plain Account of Christian Perfection.* Kansas City: Beacon Hill, 1966.

——. *Explanatory Notes on the New Testament.* London: William Bowyer, 1818. (Available from Schmul Publishing Co., Salem, OH)

Secondary Sources
Augustinian-Calvinistic Works

Calvin, John. *Institutes of the Christian Religion, Vol. 1 & 2.* Translated by Henry Beveridge, Esq.

Hodges, Charles. *Systematic Theology, Vol. 1-3.* New York: Charles Scribner's Sons, 1888.

Saint Augustine. *Nicene and Post-Nicene Fathers, Vol. 5.* Edited by Philip Schaff. The Christian Literature Co. 1887.

Neo-Calvinistic Works

Hodge, Zane. *Grace in Eclipse.* Dallas: Redencia Viva, 1985.

——. *Absolutely Free.* Grand Rapids: Zondervan, 1989.

Moody. March/April, 1996.

Wesleyan-Arminian Works

Arminius, James. *The Writings of James Arminius, Vol. 1-3.* Translated by James Nichols and W.R. Bagnell. Grand Rapids: Baker Book House, 1977.

Collins, Kenneth. *John Wesley on Salvation.* Grand Rapids: Francis Asbury Press, Zondervan, 1989.

Coppedge, Allan. *John Wesley in Theological Debate*. Wilmore, Kentucky: Wesley Heritage Press, 1987.

Cox, Leo George. *John Wesley's Concept of Perfection*. Salem: Schmul Pub., 1999.

Fletcher, John. *The Works of John Fletcher, Vol. 1-4*. Salem: Schmul Pub., 1974.

——. *John Fletcher's Checks to Antinomianism*. Abridged by Rev. Peter Wiseman. Kansas City: Beacon Hill Press, 1948.

Fuhrman, Eldon. "Wesleyan Doctrine of Grace." Delivered at the Evangelical Theological Society Annual Meeting, Reformed Theological Seminary, 1975. (Typewritten.)

Harding, Samuel R. *Eternal Security and the Bible as seen by a Layman*. Salem. OH: Schmul Pub., 1982.

Matlock, Paul. *The Four Justifications in Fletcher's Theology*. Salem, OH: Schmul Pub., 1980.

Miley, John. *Systematic Theology, Vol. 2*. Peabody, Massachusetts: Hendrickson Publishers, 1989.

Oden, Thomas. *Scriptural Christianity*. Grand Rapids: Zondervan, 1994.

Shank, Robert. *Life in the Son*. Springfield, MO: Westcott Pub., 1961.

Taylor, Richard S. *The Scandal of Pre-forgiveness*. Salem, OH: Schmul Publishing Co., 1993.

——. *A Right Conception of Sin*. Salem, OH: Schmul Publishing Co., 2002.

Thorsen, Donald. *The Wesleyan Quadrilateral*. Grand Rapids: Zondervan, 1990.

Wiley, H. Orton and Culbertson, Paul T. *Introduction to Christian Theology*. Kansas City: Beacon Hill Press, 1967.

Yocum, Dale. *Creeds in Contrast*. Salem, OH: Schmul Publishing Co., 1986.

Other Works

Morris, Leon. *The Gospel according to John* in *The New International Commentary on the New Testament*. Grand Rapids, MI: Wm. B. Eerdmans Publishing Co., 1995.

Oden, Thomas. *The Living God: Systematic Theology: Volume One*. New York: HarperCollins, 1987.

Wallace, Daniel B. *Greek Grammar Beyond the Basics: An Exegetical Syntax of the New Testament*. Grand Rapids: Zondervan, 1996.
